A Totally New Kind of Business Book!

Finally – a business book that makes the process of starting and growing a business easier.

Other business books give you advice – *The Successful Business Organizer* takes you step-by-step through all the details of getting up and running, helping you achieve your goals sooner – and successfully!

- **Checklists to guide you and remind you**
- **Comparison shopping guides**
- **Questions to ask advisors and partners**
- **Organizing tools**
- **Red Tape Warnings to help keep you out of trouble**
- **Tips and secrets to save you money**

Also by Rhonda Abrams:
- *The Successful Business Plan: Secrets & Strategies*
- *Wear Clean Underwear: Business Wisdom from Mom*

Praise for *The Successful Business Plan: Secrets & Strategies*
- One of the two best books for small business – *Forbes Magazine*
- One of the 20 best books for start-ups – *Inc. Magazine*
- One of the 20 essential books for entrepreneurs – *Home Office Computing*
- Used by leading entrepreneurs and hundreds of business schools nationwide

Praise for *Wear Clean Underwear: Business Wisdom from Mom*
- Selection, Book-of-the-Month Club
- "Full of sound business advice" – *Inc. Magazine*
- "Funny and insightful" – *Detroit Free Press*
- "Fascinating profiles of companies" – *People Magazine*

THE
SUCCESSFUL
BUSINESS
ORGANIZER

RHONDA ABRAMS
America's Most-Read Small Business Columnist

Running 'R' Media™
Palo Alto, California

The Successful Business Organizer™
© 2001 by Rhonda Abrams

Published by Running 'R' Media™

Services for our readers:

Colleges, business schools, corporate purchasing:
Running 'R' Media™ offers special discounts and supplemental class materials for universities, business schools, and corporate training. Contact: info@RhondaWorks.com or call 650-289-9120.

Updates:
Information contained in this book was current at the time of publishing. For updates, check our website, www.RhondaWorks.com and register at www.RhondaWorks.com (see below).

For more business advice and resources:
Check RhondaWorks, www.RhondaWorks.com, an interactive online business planning center that you will find very useful as you grow your business. RhondaWorks contains companion and updated information for this Organizer, and enables you to enter your personal business "To Do" list and receive regular "Reminders," keeping you on track as your business develops.

Contact us:
E-mail: info@RhondaWorks.com
Write: Running 'R' Media™
     555 Bryant Street, #180
     Palo Alto, CA 94301
Phone: 650-289-9120
Fax: 650-289-9125

Running 'R' Media™ is a division of Rhonda, Inc., a California corporation.
Visit us at www.RhondaWorks.com.

Managing Editor: Erin Wait
Cover Designer: Arthur Wait
Production Assistant: Melody Rust

ISBN: 0-9669635-3-9

"This publication is designed to provide accurate and authoritative information in regard to the subject matter covered. It is sold with the understanding that the publisher and author are not engaged in rendering legal, accounting, or other professional services. If legal advice or other expert assistance is required, the services of a competent professional person should be sought." – *from a Declaration of Principles jointly adopted by a committee of the American Bar Association and a committee of publishers.*

Printed in Canada

this business belongs to:

_____

dates to remember

started planning on:

_____

opened for business on:

_____

table of contents

worksheets & planning tools

about
rhonda abrams

Rhonda Abrams writes the nation's most widely read small business column, which appears on USATODAY.com and Inc.com, in over 130 newspapers throughout the country, and in the *Costco Connection*. In her column, Rhonda focuses on the concerns and challenges of entrepreneurs, offering common-sense advice based on solid business experience and real-life examples. This has earned her the reputation as "America's Most Trusted Small Business Advisor."

Rhonda is also the author of *The Successful Business Plan: Secrets & Strategies* and *Wear Clean Underwear: Business Wisdom from Mom.*

The Successful Business Plan was acclaimed by *Forbes, Inc., Home Office Computing,* and others as one of the best books for entrepreneurs and is used by business schools nationwide. The best-selling business plan guide, *The Successful Business Plan* has over a quarter million copies in print.

Wear Clean Underwear (Dell, 2000) examines the business practices of outstanding companies and was chosen as a Selection of the Book-of-the-Month Club, the Money Club, and the Quality Paperback Book Club. It has been translated into many languages, including Dutch, Korean, and Japanese.

Rhonda not only writes about business — she lives it! She has started three successful companies. Rhonda's experience gives her an extraordinary depth of experience and a real-life understanding of the challenges facing entrepreneurs.

Rhonda started her first company in 1986: a management consulting practice working with clients ranging from one-person startups to Fortune 500 companies. In 1995, she was an Internet pioneer, founding a web-content company for small business, which she later sold.

In 1999, Rhonda started Running 'R' Media, a publishing and content creation company focusing exclusively on topics of entrepreneurship, small business, and new business development. And in 2000, Rhonda extended her business by starting RhondaWorks, an online and offline company to assist entrepreneurs in starting and growing their companies.

A popular public speaker and lecturer, Rhonda is regularly invited to address leading industry associations, corporate events, and business schools. She was educated at Harvard University and UCLA, where she was named Outstanding Senior. Rhonda lives in Palo Alto, California.

Visit Rhonda Abrams at www.RhondaWorks.com

acknowledgements

Everything I accomplish is a result of teamwork. I am fortunate to work with exceptionally talented and committed people who help make everything we do at Running 'R' Media and RhondaWorks possible.

The greatest thanks for the development of *The Successful Business Organizer* goes to Erin Wait, the Managing Editor of Running 'R' Media. Erin's many gifts, including her intelligence, thoughtfulness, skill, and creativity, have guided the creation and development of this Organizer every step of the way and has made this book the high-quality product that it has turned out to be. With the many demands on my time, Erin has been invaluable in making Running 'R' Media a success. I appreciate her contributions and her patience.

I also want to thank Melody Rust, one of the newest additions to Running 'R' Media, for her graphic assistance on this Organizer. I look forward to working with Melody on future projects as well.

My assistant, Deborah Kaye, has had to juggle the many demands of a publishing company, a growing company, and a boss with too many things going on at once. Arthur Wait, our talented web and graphic designer, brings a wide-range of skills and good judg-ment to bear in all the many things he is asked to do, and does them all with good-natured willingness. Other members of the RhondaWorks team, including Jim Schulte and Kelny Farber, keep the wheels running, especially when I have to be busy writing.

I also want to thank the counselors and directors of Small Business Development Centers that we met with during the course of the development of this Organizer, for their input and advice. The SBDC network is one of the greatest resources for small business in the U.S.

I am also very fortunate to work closely with the Council of Better Business Bureaus, BBBOnline, and the network of local Better Business Bureaus throughout the United States. They have allowed me to use some of the fine information the BBB produces on running an ethical business, alternative dispute resolution, and customer service.

Finally, I want to thank my readers, who regularly e-mail and write me with their feedback on my books and columns. This helps give me insight into the needs and aspiration of entrepreneurs. And they keep me inspired by their enthusiasm and optimism.

letter from rhonda

Congratulations! You're engaged in one of the most exciting projects of all — growing a business. And I want to help you succeed.

Starting, changing, or growing a business can seem an overwhelming task. I know; I've done it myself. There are so many things to decide, to remember, to do. It's easy to become overwhelmed. So we've created a totally new concept in a business book — a Business Organizer.

This Organizer will:

- Help you stay on top of all the things you have to do
- Help you keep all your info and stuff together
- Give you good ideas, tips and shortcuts
- Warn you of potential problems and pitfalls
- Help you think through your decision-making process
- Help you budget and plan
- Increase your chances of success

We here at Running 'R' Media put our heads together to think through all the steps you'll need to follow when planning your new, changing, or growing company. And we've created handy tools to guide you through that process.

My previous book, *The Successful Business Plan: Secrets & Strategies,* helps you put together a "business plan," the kind of plan you'll need for getting financing or thinking through long-term strategy. But this Organizer helps you deal with the day-to-day process of getting your business up and running — all those pesky details like:

- Shopping
- Choosing a location
- Comparing options
- Coming up with marketing and sales pitches
- Keeping track of names, numbers, and information
- Figuring out what to ask consultants and advisors.

There's nothing else like this Organizer available; that's why we created it. I wish I'd had something like this to guide me when I started my own businesses. And for additional assistance, be certain to check out my website, www.RhondaWorks.com.

Don't be intimidated by how much there is in this Organizer. We tried to include as much as possible. Feel free to use the things you need and leave the ones you don't. It's your tool — use it to help you succeed.

Good luck. I'm pulling for you!

Warmly,

Rhonda

my checklist

You may be starting a new business or expanding an existing business. Either way, you'll find you need to follow a series of steps in a relatively logical order. Whether you only have a few weeks or you're looking ahead more than a year, use this checklist as a guide of "To Do's" for planning your business growth. The planning calendars that follow will help you customize your checklist to your particular situation and timeline.

STARTING MY BUSINESS

One year or earlier before launching my business:	Page
☐ Identify my personal goals	15
☐ Explore my business interests and opportunities	14, 19
☐ Start saving money to start my business	30, 106
☐ Sketch out my initial business concept	19
☐ Clarify what assets I begin with	109
☐ Make a list of my role models and why I want to emulate them	16
☐ Assess potential financial risks	31
☐ Read business books, magazines and articles	44, 78
☐ Take classes and/or get certified in my field or industry, if necessary	77
☐ Take advantage of any training my current employer offers	77
☐ Join community, entrepreneur, and/or industry groups	68
☐ Set up files	27
☐ Set up my computer files	27
☐ Improve my computer/technology skills	77
☐ Get a personal credit check	28
☐ Clean up my credit	28, 106
☐ Begin thinking of a company name	30

☐ Check out domain names   39

☐ Check out trademarks   34, 148

☐ Start keeping track of everything I spend money on   27–29

☐ Begin my business plan   24, 111

☐ Begin doing market research   44

☐ Start an initial list of my competition   51

☐ Start learning/getting comfortable with financial terms   93

☐ Start a list keeping track of all my credit cards   110

☐ Start a list keeping track of potential investors/lenders   112

☐ Ask for referrals of good business attorneys and accountants   94, 140

☐ Discuss the impact of starting a business with my family/spouse/significant other   28

Nine months to a year before launch:

☐ Buy or upgrade my own computer/printer/software   160

☐ Increase my credit lines and apply for credit cards   108

☐ Develop a simple start-up budget   30–32

☐ Set a target launch date   53

☐ List all necessary business licenses/permits   149

☐ Begin developing my company identity   30

☐ Get temporary business cards   61

☐ Decide whether I want partners   23, 140

☐ Find out the size of my market   47

☐ Identify potential strategic partners   50

☐ List potential distribution channels/distributors   130

☐ Scope out supply sources   128

☐ Schedule an initial meeting with an attorney   139

☐ Start and keep a list of important legal numbers and info I'll need to use frequently   153

☐ Research possible locations   119

Six to nine months before launch:

☐ Assemble an advisory committee   80

☐ Clarify characteristics and capabilities of my competition   51, 107

☐ Determine what others are charging   106

☐ Establish prices   104

☐ Clarify characteristics of my target market   48–49

☐ Write my elevator pitch   60

☐ Contact potential strategic partners   52

☐ Contact potential distributors   131

☐ Research potential marketing vehicles and develop a marketing program   61

☐ Start a list of milestones achieved to date and future milestones   54–55

☐ Identify potential exit strategies   24

☐ Write first draft of my business plan   233

☐ Begin developing my business budget, cash flow, and financial statements   95

☐ Schedule an initial meeting with an accountant   140

☐ Choose cash or accrual basis accounting method   102

☐ Choose a fiscal year   94

☐ Decide whether I want/need investors (after doing a preliminary budget)   24, 106

☐ Determine what form of business is best for me   139

☐ Apply for incorporation, if necessary   140

☐ Apply for necessary business licenses/permits   148–149

☐ Get a Federal Tax ID number and state Tax ID number if needed   149, 153

☐ File a "dba" with my county or other authority, if required   149, 153, 237

☐ Apply for trademarks, patents, and copyrights   148

☐ Figure out how I want to share ownership, distribute company stock   144

☐ Get all agreements in writing!!   140

☐ Establish a business banking relationship   102–103

☐ Establish regular financial review systems   93

☐ Get an accounting/bookkeeping software program   94, 102

☐ Identify technology needs   160

☐ Establish or upgrade my Internet connection   167

☐ Research and compare ISPs/website hosting options   168

☐ Attend industry trade show   62–63

☐ Plan my production and order fulfillment process   128

☐ Select a location, negotiate lease terms   120–121

☐ Find an insurance broker/agent   134, 136

☐ Take a vacation   78

Three to six months before launch:

☐ Revise my business plan and prepare Powerpoint presentation   111

☐ Revise my budgets and financial forms   95

☐ Determine salary and compensation packages for key employees   88–89

☐ Secure financing; raise money; meet with potential investors/funders   106

☐ Further develop my corporate identity and hire a graphic designer if appropriate   38

☐ Determine the purpose and functions of my website and begin designing it   169

☐ Select ISP/host of website and set up e-mail   167

☐ Conduct informal focus groups with potential customers   44, 49

☐ Refine marketing plan and marketing materials   66–67

☐ Secure initial clients or customers   72–73

☐ Secure strategic partners   50, 52

☐ Enter into distribution agreement   133

☐ Design and begin build-out of my location(s)   123

☐ Order heavy equipment; specialized furniture   122

☐ Get accounting software and devise standard financial forms, invoices, etc.   102

☐ Make a list of my regular tax and financial due-dates   114

☐ Issue press release announcing the business to any monthly publications   64–65

☐ Reserve phone numbers from the phone company   158–159

One to three months before launch:

☐ Finalize company identity, logo and colors   38

☐ Develop employee policies, such as sick leave, benefits and vacation   84–85

☐ Select a payroll service   134, 136

☐ Develop a sales pitch and prepare sales materials   73–74

☐ Get business cards, stationery, brochures, etc.   62

☐ Hire my top sales personnel/management   91

☐ Order raw materials/production materials   128

☐ Buy equipment, furniture, computers, hardware, and software   122, 160

☐ Set up shipping accounts, such as FedEx   128, 171

☐ Develop my customer service procedures and policies   176–177

☐ Get appropriate business insurance   134

Month before launch

☐ Get phones and wiring installed   159, 167

☐ Finish build-out of location/space   122

☐ Buy office supplies   126, 186

☐ Hire non-managerial/hourly employees   91

☐ Conduct employee training programs   83

☐ Buy mailing list of potential customers if appropriate   73

☐ Prepare mailing to announce launch of business   62

☐ Order advertising specialty items to distribute at open house/trade shows   62

Launch day:

☐ Send announcements and mailings   68

☐ Hold an open house or "office warming"   71

☐ Exhibit at industry trade show   63

☐ Issue a press release   64–65

GROWING MY BUSINESS

Nine Months to a Year Before Growth Milestone

Six to Nine Months Before Growth Milestone

Three to Six Months Before Growth Milestone

One to Three Months Before Growth Milestone

Growth Milestone and Launch

GOALS FOR STARTING MY BUSINESS

Specific Goals:

Enter the number or amount you hope to achieve for your business in one year, five years, and ten years.

	One Year	Five Years	Ten Years
Number of Employees			
Number of Locations			
Annual Sales			
Profits or Profit Margin			
Number of Products/Services			
Awards/Recognition Received			
Ownership Allocation			
Other:			

Priorities:

Rate your priorities for your business.

	Urgent	Important	I'll get to it sooner or later	Not on the radar screen	Not applicable to my business
Add Employees	☐	☐	☐	☐	☐
Add New Lines	☐	☐	☐	☐	☐
Increase Marketing	☐	☐	☐	☐	☐
Add Locations	☐	☐	☐	☐	☐
Add Capacity	☐	☐	☐	☐	☐
Increase Salaries	☐	☐	☐	☐	☐
Increase Inventory	☐	☐	☐	☐	☐
Increase Profits	☐	☐	☐	☐	☐
Retire Debts	☐	☐	☐	☐	☐
Increase Reserve	☐	☐	☐	☐	☐
Acquire Other Companies	☐	☐	☐	☐	☐
Other:					
_____	☐	☐	☐	☐	☐
_____	☐	☐	☐	☐	☐
_____	☐	☐	☐	☐	☐
_____	☐	☐	☐	☐	☐

GOALS FOR GROWING MY BUSINESS

Specific Goals:

Enter the number or amount you hope to achieve for your business in one year, five years, and ten years.

	One Year	Five Years	Ten Years
Number of Employees			
Number of Locations			
Annual Sales			
Profits or Profit Margin			
Number of Products/Services			
Awards/Recognition Received			
Ownership Allocation			
Other:			

Priorities:

Rate your priorities for your business.

	Urgent	Important	I'll get to it sooner or later	Not on the radar screen	Not applicable to my business
Add Employees	☐	☐	☐	☐	☐
Add New Lines	☐	☐	☐	☐	☐
Increase Marketing	☐	☐	☐	☐	☐
Add Locations	☐	☐	☐	☐	☐
Add Capacity	☐	☐	☐	☐	☐
Increase Salaries	☐	☐	☐	☐	☐
Increase Inventory	☐	☐	☐	☐	☐
Increase Profits	☐	☐	☐	☐	☐
Retire Debts	☐	☐	☐	☐	☐
Increase Reserve	☐	☐	☐	☐	☐
Acquire Other Companies	☐	☐	☐	☐	☐
Other:					
	☐	☐	☐	☐	☐
	☐	☐	☐	☐	☐
	☐	☐	☐	☐	☐
	☐	☐	☐	☐	☐

BUSINESS PLANNING CALENDAR

January, 20___

February, 20___

May, 20___

June, 20___

September, 20___

October, 20___

BUSINESS PLANNING CALENDAR

March, 20___

April, 20___

July, 20___

August, 20___

November, 20___

December, 20___

BUSINESS PLANNING CALENDAR

Month:_____, 20___

Sunday	Monday	Tuesday	Wednesday	Thursday	Friday	Saturday

BUSINESS PLANNING CALENDAR

Month:_____, 20___

Sunday	Monday	Tuesday	Wednesday	Thursday	Friday	Saturday

MY SHOPPING LIST

my vision

When you imagine your business, what do you hope for? To make a lot of money? Use your creativity? Have more flexibility in your life? Do you see yourself working alone or building a company with other employees? Do you hope your company grows very large or do you want it to stay small?

Some entrepreneurs describe themselves as "visionaries" because they can conceive of grand schemes, bold new inventions, vast improvements on existing products. They can envision their companies clobbering the competition, defining new product categories, perhaps growing to hundreds of millions, if not billions of dollars.

But a business "vision" doesn't have to be so revolutionary to succeed (indeed, you may be even more likely to succeed if your goals are somewhat less ambitious). A business vision is the ability to articulate what you see your business becoming — what it will do or make, how it will grow and compete, how big it will get. You may already have a pretty good sense of your business vision, or perhaps all those details are fuzzy. You know you want to be your own boss, but you don't know what form the business should take.

Coming up with your business vision can be one of the most exciting aspects of starting or expanding a business. This is the stage between having a "dream"

and having a "plan." It's when you get to explore your personal motivations, your business creativity, and how your own values intersect with your business goals. It's an exciting but challenging time. This chapter helps you see and articulate your business vision more clearly.

WHAT MOTIVATES ME?

What are your personal goals in growing your business? Its success may depend on answering this question.

Some businesses fail, and others flounder, because their founders or executives are uncertain what they really want to achieve, and they don't structure the company and their responsibilities in ways that satisfy their personal needs and ambitions.

The Four C's

For most entrepreneurs, these goals can be summed up in what I call the Four C's: Creativity, Control, Challenge, and Cash. Of course, we each want all four of these to some degree, but knowing which we want or need most can help us structure our companies to best achieve our goals.

For instance, my very first clients were the owners of a small sportswear apparel company. The woman began the business because she was good at — and loved — designing clothes. Her primary motivation was being able to act on her creativity. But an apparel company doesn't run on designs alone. There are a myriad of purely "business" aspects of the company — sales, operations, manufacturing, etc. If she hadn't planned for it, she might have spent the majority of her time on such issues instead of designing. Fortunately, she had a partner to take over those responsibilities. She gave up some control — which wasn't a major concern of hers — to maintain her creativity.

Which of the Four C's motivates you most?

- **Creativity.** Entrepreneurs want to leave their mark. Their companies are not only a means of making a living, but a way of creating something that bears their stamp. Creativity comes in many forms, from designing or making a new "thing," to devising a new business process, or even a new way to make sales, handle customers, or reward employees.

  If you have a high need for creativity, make certain you remain involved in the creative process as your company develops. You'll want to shape your business so it's not just an instrument for earning an income but also a way for maintaining your creative stimulation and making a larger contribution to society. But don't overpersonalize your company, especially if it's large. Allow room for others, particularly partners and key personnel, to share in the creative process.

- **Control.** Most of us start businesses because we want more control over our own lives. Perhaps we want more control over how our good ideas are implemented. Perhaps we want, or need, more control of our work hours or conditions so we can be more involved in family, community, or even golf! Control is a major motivator for most entrepreneurs — usually more important than money. But how much control you need — especially on a day-to-day basis — directly influences how large your company can be.

If you need or want a great deal of control over your time, you'll most likely need to keep your company smaller. In a large company, you have less immediate control over many decisions. If you're a person who needs control, you can still grow your business larger. You'll need to structure communication and reporting systems to ensure that you have sufficient information about and direction over developments to give you personal satisfaction. If you seek outside funding in the form of investors, understand the nature of control your funders will have and be certain you are comfortable with these arrangements.

- **Challenge.** If you're starting or expanding a business, it's clear you like challenge — at least to some degree. You're likely to be a problem-solver and risk-taker, enjoying the task of figuring out solutions to problems or devising new undertakings. Challenge-hungry entrepreneurs can be some of the most successful businesspeople, but they can also be their own worst enemies — flitting from one thing to another, never focusing long enough to succeed.

  If you have a high need for challenge in your business life, it's important to develop positive means to meet this need, especially once your company is established and the initial challenge of starting a company is met. Otherwise, you may find yourself continually starting new projects that divert attention from your company's overall goals. As you plan your company, establish personal goals that not only provide you with sufficient stimulation, but also advance — rather than distract from — the growth of your business. (Or take up sky diving on the side!)

- **Cash.** Every entrepreneur wants to make money. Perhaps it's just enough money to provide a decent income; perhaps it's so much money you can buy a jet. How much you want or need affects how you'll develop your business. Will you need investors and when? Will you sacrifice control to grow the business quickly?

Keep in mind there are sometimes trade-offs between personal goals: wanting more cash often means having less control; staying at the center of the creative

MY PERSONAL GOALS: THE FOUR C'S

Make copies of this worksheet for yourself and your partners or key employees, if any. Check the level of importance to you in each area.

	Extremely Important	Somewhat Important	Somewhat Unimportant	Not Important
Creativity				
Determining the design or look of products/packaging				
Creating new products or services				
Devising new business procedures/policies				
Identifying new company opportunities				
Creating new business materials				
Devising new ways of doing "old" things				
Other:				
Control				
Over own work responsibilities				
Over own time, work hours, etc.				
Over company decisions and directions				
Over products/services				
Over other employees				
Over work environment				
Over social/environmental impact of products/services				
Over own future and business' future				
Other:				
Challenge				
Long-term problem solving				
Critical problem solving (putting out fires)				
Handling many issues at one time				
Continually dealing with new issues				
Perfecting solutions, products or services				
Organizing diverse projects and keeping the group goal-focused				
Other:				

Cash

List approximate dollar ranges for the following. Measure wealth as the value of stocks or of the company.

Income needed currently _____   Wealth desired in 2–5 years _____

Income desired in 12–24 months _____   Wealth desired in 6–10 years _____

Income desired in 2–5 years _____   Wealth desired 10+ years _____

MY ROLE MODELS

Use this space to list the names of people you admire, whether they're in business or not.

Name and Job or Role	What traits of theirs do you admire?	How could you incorporate those traits in your business?

process may mean you need to have a partner or grow slowly, once again trading off control or cash. Examine your personal goals and those of key personnel using The Four C's worksheet on page 15.

WHAT INSPIRES ME?

At some point in their business lives, all entrepreneurs are inspired — by an idea, a person, or an opportunity. That inspiration not only gets you started; it also keeps you going.

Use the pages of this organizer to record the initial spark that set you on this journey. You may reach a point down the road when you ask yourself, "Why did I start all this?" Re-read what you've written here when you need to be "re-inspired," or just to get a reminder of what your goals were from the beginning.

The worksheets in this section are also the starting point for articulating your business concept and identifying your niche market and customer base.

My Role Models

Do you want to be another Bill Gates? Do you see yourself as a future Oprah Winfrey? Or do you look up to your uncle who ran his own store or your older sister who has been self-employed for ten years?

Many of us are fortunate enough to have people in business whom we admire or would like to emulate. You may know them personally, or you may have read about their business practices or success.

Thinking about your role models can help you clarify your own business vision. If your business hero is Bill Gates, what is it about him that you admire? His ability to make a great deal of money? Build a huge business? His marketing and strategic capabilities? Or do you admire his technical knowledge?

Take a moment to think about who your business role models are and why by completing the "My Role Models" worksheet on page 16.

My Business Values

As we build our companies, we have goals not only for what our business will help us achieve for ourselves, but also how our business will impact others: our employees, customers, the environment, our communities.

Some of the specific ways to do that are discussed in the chapter "Good Company," but right from the start — as you look at your business vision — it's also a good time to think about what values you want to incorporate into your business.

For many entrepreneurs, the business values they want their company to project are part of their inspiration for getting started in the first place. Incorporating your values into your business will help you build a company that gives you greater satisfaction in the long term, and quite possibly, a more successful company as well. Having a company that ascribes to and practices certain positive values can be a competitive advantage in attracting and retaining employees and developing customer loyalty.

Be cautious, however, that as you build your business around your values, you do not impose your personal beliefs (especially religious or political beliefs) on others.

To help clarify the values you'd like to incorporate into your business, use the "My Business Values" worksheet on page 18.

My "Bright Idea"

What excites you about your business idea? If you have two or three ideas, what do you like best about each one? Where did the idea come from? How has it evolved since you started the process of turning the idea into a business?

By looking at how you initially got the inspiration for your business, you can take the next step towards determining how you might get others excited about your business also. That's the start of taking an idea and turning it into a plan, which becomes a successful business. Use the worksheet on page 20 to describe what you like about your business idea.

MY BUSINESS VALUES

Describe what values are important to you in building your company as they relate to:

Corporate culture and nature of the work environment (management/employee relations and communication, work hours and flexibility, dress code, office location, décor, etc.):

Business Ethics (customer treatment; relations with vendors, distributors, competitors; advertising, etc.):

Employee Treatment (wages and benefits, lay-off policies, promotions, empowerment, etc):

Community and Civic Involvement:

The Environment:

Other:

WHAT IS MY BUSINESS CONCEPT?

Meeting needs is the basis of all business. You can devise a wonderful new machine, but if it doesn't address some real and important need or desire, people won't buy it, and your business will fail. Even Thomas Edison recognized this fact when he said, "Anything that won't sell, I don't want to invent."

Now that you know what your spark and passion is about your idea, use the worksheet on page 21 to determine how your product or service will meet new or existing needs in the marketplace.

The success of a concept often hinges on whether it does something newer or better than anyone else. Being new or better can take many forms:

- **Something New.** This could be a new product, service, feature, or technology.

- **Something Better.** This could be an improvement on an existing product or service encompassing more features, lower price, greater reliability, faster speed, increased convenience, or enhanced technology.

- **An Underserved or New Market.** This is a market for which there is greater demand than competitors can currently satisfy, an unserved location, or a small part of an overall market — a niche market — that hasn't yet been dominated by other competitors. Sometimes, markets become underserved when large companies abandon or neglect smaller portions of their current customer base.

- **New Delivery System or Distribution Channel.** New technologies, particularly the Internet, allow companies to reach customers more efficiently. This has opened up many new opportunities for businesses to provide products or services less expensively, to a wider geographic area, or with far greater choice.

- **Increased Integration.** This occurs when a product is both manufactured and sold by the same company, or when a company offers more services or products in one location.

Your concept should be strong in at least one area. If not, you should ask yourself how your company will be truly competitive. The "Business Concept" worksheet on page 21 helps you evaluate your basic business idea.

Once you have considered your business concept, values, and motivations, try writing a mission statement for your business. You will likely write and rewrite this several times, not only before you start your business, but after it is well underway. Still, it is a good exercise as you clarify and articulate your business vision to write one now. The worksheet "My Mission Statement" on page 22 will get you started.

WHO DO I WANT TO WORK WITH?

Nothing affects your day-to-day work life more than the people you work with. Yes, work can be meaningful if you have challenging tasks, play with cool technology, or make lots money, but whether you feel like getting out of bed in the morning depends most on who you're going to work with that day. So if you're going to run your own business, you might as well try to work with people you like.

You may not be eager to work with anyone else. You may want to be completely in charge of your own life and not have to deal with the distractions of having other people around. Or you may feel you have no choice other than working alone since your potential business can't sustain the income to hire others.

But even if you plan to work alone, in reality, you'll still work with many others: your customers or clients, vendors, distributors, referral sources. Perhaps you'll work with them over the phone or through e-mail rather than in person, but they can still make or break your day. You may even find yourself "working" with people you would never have considered your co-workers, like the after-school babysitter who watches your kids while you work in your home office.

When you structure your business, think carefully about who you want to work with and why. This is

MY 'BRIGHT IDEA'

Use this space to record your initial business idea(s). This will become a starting point for defining your business concept and why it can be competitive in the marketplace, on the next page. It will also be useful as you prepare your marketing materials and write your "Elevator Pitch," described on page 60.

What is your business idea?

How did you come up with it?

What excites you about it?

MY BUSINESS CONCEPT

Using this worksheet as a guide, outline your business concept as you presently envision it. Refer to the description of each area on page 19 for more information. For your Mission Statement, on the following worksheet, condense this concept into a single sentence.

In what ways will your business offer:

New Products or Services:

Improved Features/Services and Added Value:

New or Underserved Markets Reached:

New or Improved Delivery or Distribution Method:

Methods of Increased Integration:

MY MISSION STATEMENT

Use this worksheet to brainstorm possible mission statements for your business. For example, a finished Mission Statement might read:

"AAA, Inc., is a spunky, imaginative food products and service company aimed at offering high-quality, moderately priced, occasionally unusual foods using only natural ingredients. We view ourselves as partners with our customers, our employees, our community, and our environment, and we take personal responsibility in our actions towards each. We aim to become a regionally recognized brand name, capitalizing on the sustained interest in Southwestern and Mexican food. Our goal is moderate growth, annual profitability, and maintaining our sense of humor."

Describe the following in one sentence:

Core business concept:
Core business values:
Core business goals:
Core financial goals:
Corporate culture:

Now take a stab at combining these sentences into one comprehensive mission statement. You will revisit and rewrite it several times, but you'll need a mission statement for your business plan, investors, employees, and others, so get something on paper now.

_____

_____

_____

_____

_____

especially true if you're taking on partners, investors, or employees. These are the people who'll not only affect your mood but your bottom line as well. They may share, or even control, ownership of your company. Spend time getting to know the people you'll work with most. Find out whether their goals, work style, and values fit yours.

Partners

If you are going to take on a partner, carefully consider why you want or need one. As you start your business, you may feel uncertain about being on your own, but that feeling of uncertainty may pass quickly. A partner will be around for a long, long time. Remember, partners own a piece of the business. Even if you bring in someone with only a minority interest as a partner, your future is tied to them.

Make certain your expectations of what you'll get out of a partnership are realistic. Are they willing to work as hard as you? Do they bring the same level of talent or skill (although perhaps in a different area) as you? Do they have the same long-term view of where they want the business to be?

You have more leeway, legally, to ask questions of potential partners than of employees. Of course, make certain your potential partner is honest, but also examine their personal attitudes, family responsibilities that have an impact on their attention, how they handle stress, how much money they need and how soon, and any other personal issues that may affect your working relationship.

The best way to take on a partner is with clear-cut definitions of responsibilities and authority. It's nice to believe you will make every decision together, but that's not realistic. Who, in the end, gets to call the shots? And be careful about going to work with a friend — often it's both the business and the friendship that suffers.

QUESTIONS TO ASK . . . A POTENTIAL PARTNER

- Why are you going into business?
- What are your personal goals for this business?
- How much money do you need now? How much money will you need over the next 12 months? 24 months? 36 months?
- How much money are you able and willing to invest in the company, if any?
- How big a company would you like this to be one day?
- How much time do you have to devote to the business?
- What other obligations do you have, both business and personal, that will affect your commitment of time, money and attention?
- How do you see decisions being made? By whom?
- What areas of responsibility do you feel capable of taking on?
- What areas of responsibility do you want to be in charge of?
- How formal or informal do you like to be about such things as work hours, dress code, etc.?
- Is your family supportive of this commitment?
- Have you ever been in a partnership before? What happened?
- What are your fears in this partnership?

See also the worksheet on "Discussing Partnership Terms" on page 141.

When taking on a partner, be absolutely certain to get a written agreement, specifying how you can buy each other (or the other's heirs) out of the business. A messy "divorce" from a business partner is as difficult as a messy marital divorce — with potentially greater financial consequences. Drawing up an agreement now may avoid difficulties if you later decide to go your separate ways.

Use the guide "Questions to Ask...A Potential Partner" on page 23 to discuss the nature of your relationship before you sign any agreements.

Investors

You are tied to your investors for the life of your business, so proceed carefully. When you need money, of course, you may feel lucky to get the money you need from anyone. But over time, if you have a fearful, intrusive, or controlling investor, you may soon regret being involved with them. And there usually isn't an easy way out.

It's unlikely you can ask as many probing questions of a potential investor as you can a potential partner because you'll be concerned about scaring them away. And investors usually view the investment process as an examination of you — not the other way round. Nevertheless, you want to spend as much time as you can getting to know your potential investors. Find out if they've invested in other companies before. If so, speak to the other entrepreneurs who've worked with them. What are their financial and business motivations for investing? Are those goals a good fit with your own? How much control do they want in the business?

Use the guide, "Questions to Ask...A Potential Investor" below to help clarify whether an investor is a good fit for you.

The section of this Organizer on Money discusses in more detail the types of investors you might seek, and how to secure an investment. It also includes a worksheet for tracking and comparing your meetings with interested investors. If you do seek outside funding for your business, you will need a business plan. An outline for a business plan is included on page 233 of this Organizer. For detailed help in writing a winning plan, use my book, *The Successful Business Plan: Secrets and Strategies.*

WHAT IS MY EXIT PLAN?

When you're building a business, you don't spend a lot of time envisioning how you'll eventually get out of it. Oh, maybe you think one day you'll make

QUESTIONS TO ASK . . . A POTENTIAL INVESTOR

- Why are you investing in this business?
- What aspect of this business is most appealing to you?
- What other businesses have you invested in before?
- May I call some entrepreneurs you've invested with before?
- How soon do you expect to see a return on this investment?
- How would it affect you if you were to lose the money you're investing?
- If you felt I was not capable of building this company to the stage you'd like, what would you do?
- How do you see decisions being made? By whom?
- What role do you want, if any, in the company (e.g. board membership, etc.)
- Do you understand all the risks in making this investment?

enough money to retire, but while you can envision yourself golfing or gardening, what's happened to your company? You need an "exit plan."

An exit plan is a long-term strategy for transferring ownership of your company to others. "Whoa, Rhonda," I imagine you saying. "I hardly know what I'm going to be doing next month. Why should I figure out what I'm going to do with my company 10 or 20 years from now?"

If you're looking for an investor in your company, you have to spell out an exit. After all, they want to know how they're going to get their money back. If there is more than one partner in the business, having a clear exit strategy reduces the friction that comes from unspoken exit assumptions.

Even if you own the company yourself and hope to have it last through the ages, an exit plan helps direct the growth of your company. If, for instance, you would ideally like to be acquired by a larger company, you might target your product development and marketing efforts in ways that complement rather than compete with that company.

There are a number of ways you can exit your company or have the value of the company become liquid:

- **Sell.** This is often the simplest way to get value out. All types of companies can be sold, not just retail or manufacturing enterprises. Professional practices are 'bought into' by new partners, or a one-person consulting business can be sold to someone who wants a built-in customer base.

- **Be acquired.** Your company may be a good fit for a larger company that wants the part of the market, capabilities, or technologies you have developed.

- **Merge.** This is similar to being acquired but the assets of the merging companies form a new entity.

- **"Go public."** When you issue shares in your company that are traded in a stock market — an

initial public offering (IPO) — it is referred to as "going public." This doesn't necessarily mean you depart from management of the company, but you now have a way to get money for your ownership interest by selling some of your personal shares.

- **Have family members take over.** When Levi Strauss started selling blue jeans, he probably didn't envision a family-owned company bearing his name 150 years later. Even if you know you'd like this to happen, you need a plan. Your family members might not want to or be capable of running the company.

- **Employee buy-out.** An excellent way to keep your company together and to retain the jobs you've created is to structure a way for either key management or employees as a whole to buy the company. An "ESOP" — Employee Stock Ownership Plan — can help them finance the purchase and give you the cash you need

- **Go out of business.** This is the simplest (assuming you have no debts or major employee commitments), but you also get the least financial reward. But sometimes, you just want to close up shop and get on with the rest of your life.

Summary

If you were building a house, before you drew up the blueprints, laid the foundation, or even bought the land, you'd first have a vision of what you'd want that house to be: big or small, one story or two, in the city or in the country. You'd have a "vision" of your future home. The same is true when building a company: you need a vision of what you hope you'll achieve.

Over time, your business vision will almost certainly change. As you gain experience and confidence, your personal goals may evolve, and the things that seem most important to you now may be much less so in the next few years. Nevertheless, a vision is a good starting point as you go about building your company.

MY WILD IDEAS FOR MY BUSINESS

getting started

The best way to start is to start.

Starting any new, big project can seem overwhelming. There's so much to do, so many things to think about. Some of the challenges are fun: figuring out a name for your business, creating new products, thinking up innovative marketing ideas. Some of the tasks don't seem such fun: figuring out a budget, going to a lawyer, getting business licenses.

With so many things to do, it's easy to forget or overlook some of the most important things. You can get so excited about the more interesting challenges that you lose track of the mundane matters you have to attend to. In this chapter, I'll help you keep track of some of the basics and get organized so you don't lose information you'll need later.

On a more creative note, in this chapter I'll also get you started on one of the most challenging, and creative aspects of your business — forming your company identity: name, image, logo, tagline, etc. This can be very exciting, but it can also seem paralyzing because it's so important and personal.

Much of what is mentioned in this chapter is discussed in more detail later. But they're included here because you have to deal with them — at least briefly — as you get underway. I've listed some of the most important things in the "Don't Forget" checklist on page 28.

HOW DO I GET ORGANIZED?

The first and most important step in getting organized is to create a plan of what you have to do and a central place to keep track of your business-related information.

Trust me: you're about to get a lot of stuff. Whether you're starting a new business or planning changes in an existing business, you're quickly going to accumulate a whole lot of tangible stuff (reports, brochures, samples, contracts) as well as intangible stuff (information, data, advice, prices, etc.) You'll be gathering information on customers, competitors, suppliers, distributors. You'll be researching and evaluating computer hardware and software, facilities, and vendors. You'll be given names and numbers of people who can help you. And you'll be spending money — money you can later deduct as business expenses IF you keep track of it and keep receipts.

All this stuff can overwhelm you. Instead of feeling like you're making progress, you'll feel completely over your head. And if you don't stay on top of your stuff, it can directly affect your chance of success — and your bottom line!

Set up both physical files — to hold all that tangible stuff, including receipts — and digital files on your

MY "DON'T FORGET" CHECKLIST

As you get underway, there are a few things that are tempting to put off, especially because most of these will cost some money. All of these items are discussed in more detail later in the Organizer. But don't forget how important they are as you're getting started, and don't forget to figure these into your initial budget.

☐ **One or two hour consultation with a lawyer.** A few hundred dollars spent on a lawyer now is much cheaper than getting in trouble later.

☐ **A consultation with an accountant.** An accountant can advise you on tax implications and basic accounting practices.

☐ **A credit check on yourself.** Expect to use your personal credit (or give personal guarantees) for many business-related credit needs. So get a credit report, make certain everything is accurate, and correct any inaccurate or outdated information.

☐ **Business cards, mailings, or advertisements.** Let people know you're in business. Get business cards right away, even before you're in business. Don't worry that you don't have the company name or correct address. You'll want a card to leave with people you meet during your planning process.

☐ **Business licenses, permit fees, applications.**

☐ **Memberships, credentials, or certifications.** You may need to get certified, take classes, pass tests, or join professional associations to be qualified, or at least competitive, in your field. You may also want to join industry or trade associations and attend trade shows to see potential customers, suppliers, or competitors.

☐ **Budget for transportation and travel.** You're going to be going places: meeting with people, lining up customers or strategic partners, doing research, attending trade shows.

☐ **Sufficient computing power.** If you don't already have a computer, you'll need one for your business, and if you have an older computer, you'll need a new one sooner than you think.

☐ **Online access.** If you don't already have access to the Internet, you'll need it, as well as an e-mail address. Don't worry if you haven't yet chosen your domain name (see page 39) or a permanent e-mail address; you'll need some way, at least temporarily, for people to e-mail you. Some companies provide free Internet access: check www.RhondaWorks.com for sources.

☐ **A family discussion.** When you start a business or begin any new project, it has an impact on everyone around you, especially your family. You'll probably make more financial sacrifices, have less time, and have more things on your mind than before you started. If you're married, owning a business may have legal and/or tax implications for your spouse. Sit down and fully discuss your plans — the opportunities, risks, and sacrifices.

computer to hold all that intangible stuff: your notes, contact info, price comparisons, etc. You can keep a lot of that information in this Organizer, but as you gather more data, or begin on your written business plan, it's easier just to put it in the appropriate file. Otherwise, those piles of paper will just get larger and larger and larger....

Page 231 contains file folder labels you can cut out and use to set up your physical filing system. You can also use these headings as a guide to set up files and folders on your computer to help you better organize your data.

Make a note of the sources and date of any information you find. This is particularly important for data that you'll use in your business plan, like statistics on your market or competition, and it's also important to make a note of things like who gave you the name of a potential supplier, for instance, in case you later have to contact them with questions.

In addition, I'd recommend getting a good size box (like a large plastic storage tub) to keep all your bulkier items (such as samples, large brochures, research studies) in one place and easily retrievable.

My Company's Vital Statistics

Right from the beginning, start recording all important dates, numbers, and data relating to your company, such as the date of your incorporation and your federal tax identification number. You'll discover you have to refer to these again and again once you're in business, and it's annoying to have to dig through files to find the same information repeated-

ly. A place to centrally locate all vital statistics about your business is located in the Legal Chapter on page 153.

Start an Address Book

People who do not seem particularly important during the early stages of your business may be very useful at a later date. It's a horrible feeling to realize a few months down the road that you met the perfect supplier or distributor, or the person who could introduce you to the right venture capitalist, but you've lost the little slip of paper with their name, phone number, and e-mail address. That's why pages 226–229 of this Organizer offer a place to list those names as you come across them. But you will want to transfer those names to a more formal contact database or address book program on your computer as well. You never know when you might meet that "angel" who helps get your business off the ground.

CAN I MAKE MONEY?

If you are starting a new business — or growing a new part of your business — the thing that is most important for you to know before you get too far along is, "Can I Make Money?"

In addition to your formal budgeting and financial forecasts — indeed at the very beginning of your business planning — take a quick, back-of-the-napkin assessment of the realistic financial outlook for

WHAT WOULD RHONDA DO... TO GET ORGANIZED

- Set up physical and computer files to keep track of information
- Get a plastic storage tub for bulky items
- Use this Organizer to record info, contacts, and my company's vital data
- Record the date, source, and contact person for all information I collect
- Use an address list and set up a database to keep track of people and companies
- Check www.RhondaWorks.com for other organizing tips

RED TAPE ALERT!

The IRS does not necessarily allow you to claim all expenses you incur when starting your business as single-year deductions. Rather, some or all of them must be amortized over a number of years. In other words, if a particular cost must be amortized over five years, then you can only deduct one-fifth of your start-up costs in your first year. And this is only allowed if those start-up costs actually result in an operational business.

your undertaking. Use the worksheet on page 31 to give you an overview of your financial prospects.

HOW MUCH MONEY DO I NEED TO START?

I once saw a television show in which the lead character inherited $100,000 and then used it to start a business. The first thing she did was spend $75,000 on high-priced offices and fancy furniture. Fortunately, this was fiction.

During your early years in business, your top priority is to put your business dollars where they can bring you income. We'd all like to have fancy offices, but it may be more important to send out a mailing or join an industry association.

Start with a simple budget to get a sense of how much you'll need. You'll need enough money to get you through the start-up phase: researching, buying equipment, hiring help, consulting lawyers, etc. If you're going to be giving up your "day job," you'll also need to figure in enough money to meet your personal and/or family expenses.

As you gather more information about your business, you'll develop more thorough and sophisticated financial statements. Many, if not most, businesses are not funded all at once. The Simple Start-Up Budget, on page 32, gives you a place to start, but it will not be the basis of your total financing package.

Once you have an estimate of your start-up costs, you can then figure out whether you personally have sufficient money to start (from savings, investments, a spouse's income, or even from pre-sales) or

whether you're going to need to find investors or apply for a loan. In the Money chapter, you'll learn more about the nature of the sources of capital, the pros and cons of each type, and how to put together a more sophisticated budget for financing purposes. You'll also find a budgeting tool at my website, www.RhondaWorks.com, which can help you do initial budgeting projections.

HOW DO I CREATE MY COMPANY IDENTITY?

Whether you're budgeting your start-up costs or looking for funding, an important part of getting started is creating your company identity. Your company name and logo make your business feel "real," both to you and to potential customers and investors. Creating an identity can be done on the cheap, or cost thousands of dollars. I've gone both routes.

Your corporate identity helps customers remember you, understand what you do, and even develop a certain feeling about you. Your identity is your brand image.

The key elements to a corporate identity are:

- Your name
- Tagline, if any
- Logo

Once you've developed a certain identity, you'll use those elements consistently and repeatedly — on your business cards, stationery, signs, vehicles, uniforms, website. Your corporate identity is so important, you may want to use the services of a graphic designer to help you create one.

CAN I MAKE MONEY: A QUICK ASSESSMENT

Examine whether the market is large enough to bring you sufficient sales. Then estimate the total amount (gross sales) you can reasonably expect to make. The worksheets in the Marketing and Money chapters will give you a more detailed picture of your financial prospects.

Market factors:

Estimated size of my market:	
Estimated number of competitors in my market:	
Estimated growth or decline in my market:	
Realistic assessment of the opportunity in my market: ☐ outstanding ☐ good ☐ moderate ☐ poor	
Estimated number of units sold/clients served in my market per month:	
Is this number growing or declining?	
Estimated number of competitors in my market:	
Estimated number of units sold/clients served per competitor per month:	
Other market factors:	

Gross Sales Projections:

1. Realistic estimate of number of units I will sell or clients I'll serve per month:	
2. Realistic estimate of amount of average gross sales amount (total sale amount not including tax) per unit sold or client served:	$
3. Total amount of gross sales per month: (multiply line 1 by line 2)	$

Now, estimate whether you can make enough profit on those projected sales by figuring the costs involved.

Per Unit sold/Per Client, estimate :

4. Direct cost of goods/supplies:	$
5. Sales commissions:	$
6. Overhead: *(to get this figure, divide your realistic total monthly costs for overhead, e.g., rent, salaries, marketing, research, etc., by the number of units sold/clients served to figure an estimated cost per unit/client)*	$
7. Add lines 4, 5, and 6	$
8. Multiply by the number of units sold monthly (line 1)	$

Total sales per month (line 3)	$
Minus total costs (line 8)	$
Profit, before taxes, if any:	$

SIMPLE START-UP BUDGET

Use this budget to figure out the expenses you'll incur when starting your new business or project. This should cover you and your business until you are able to break even or raise another round of funding.

BUSINESS			PERSONAL	
EXPENSE	START-UP COST	MONTHLY COST	EXPENSE	MONTHLY COST
Rent / Lease			Rent / Mortgage	
Equipment / Furniture			Food (incl. dining out)	
Office Supplies			Telephone	
Telephone			Internet Service	
Internet Service			Utilities	
Utilities (incl. deposits)			Medical / Dental Exp.	
Postage and Shipping			Insurance	
Advertising / Promotion			Education	
Printing / Copying			Entertainment / Hobbies	
Licenses / Permits			Travel / Vacation	
Dues / Subscriptions			Transportation / Auto	
Auto / Transportation			Child Care	
Insurance			Cleaners / Laundry	
Loan Repayments			Pets	
Travel			Gifts	
Entertainment			Charity / Contributions	
Inventory			Loan Repayments	
Maintenance / Repairs			Other Household Exp.	
Staff / Officer Salaries				
Your Salary [from right]			**TOTAL SALARY REQ'D**	
Payroll Taxes				
Other Taxes				
Employee Benefits				
Legal, accounting, consulting fees				
Cost of Goods				
Unanticipated Costs				
TOTAL				
Estimated First Year Business Income			Cash Available from Savings and Other	
Cash Available from Savings and Other			Other Household Income (this year)	

START-UP BUDGET – SAMPLE

Sample Budget for Web Designers, Inc.

BUSINESS			PERSONAL	
EXPENSE	START-UP COST	MONTHLY COST	EXPENSE	MONTHLY COST
Rent / Lease	5,000	2,000	Rent / Mortgage	1,200
Equipment / Furniture	6,500	500	Food (incl. dining out)	650
Office Supplies	850	400	Telephone	100
Telephone	2,000	200	Internet Service	35
Internet Service	2,000	200	Utilities	150
Utilities (incl. deposits)	1,750	250	Medical / Dental Exp.	200
Postage and Shipping	800	300	Insurance	250
Advertising / Promotion	2,500	500	Education	n/a
Printing / Copying	750	200	Entertainment / Hobbies	150
Licenses / Permits	1,500	450	Travel / Vacation	150
Dues / Subscriptions	1,850	200	Transportation / Auto	350
Auto / Transportation	5,500	1,500	Child Care	365
Insurance	2,500	1,250	Cleaners / Laundry	50
Loan Repayments	1,200	1,200	Pets	75
Travel	3,000	750	Gifts	150
Entertainment	1,500	500	Charity / Contributions	75
Inventory	5,000	2,000	Loan Repayments	400
Maintenance / Repairs	500	350	Other Household Exp.	150
Staff / Officer Salaries	8,000	8,000		
Your Salary [from right]		4,500	**TOTAL SALARY REQ'D**	4,500
Payroll Taxes	2,500	2,500		
Other Taxes	1,000	500		
Employee Benefits	2,000	1,250		
Legal, accounting, consulting fees	4,000	1,200		
Cost of Goods	1,500	500		
Unanticipated Costs	3,000	1,500		
TOTAL	**66,700**	**32,700**		
Estimated First Year Business Income		30,000	Cash Available from Savings and Other	3,500
Cash Available from Savings and Other		50,000	Other Household Income (this year)	18,500

What Will I Call My Business?

I collect cute business names: "All You Knead," (a bakery), "The Barking Lot" (a dog groomer), "Shear Ecstasy" (a hair salon). A clever business name can be an excellent marketing tool, making your company immediately memorable, but coming up with a good name can seem frustrating. Big companies spend thousands of dollars researching names, and sometimes even they fail. When General Motors introduced the Chevy Nova into Latin America, it flopped. In Spanish, "No va" means "doesn't go."

In small companies, YOU are the brand, and usually the best name for your company is your own, perhaps adding a descriptive phrase to clarify what you do. My first business was called "Abrams Business Strategies" since I developed business and marketing plans.

A good company name achieves several goals:

- **Conveys the correct information.** You don't want anything in your business name that leaves potential customers confused about what you do. This can be harder than it seems: "ABC Mediation Services" may provide both mediation and arbitration, potentially confusing some clients. A very clear company name, "Prepaid Legal Services" immediately lets customers know what to expect (but watch out if your services later change or if you run into trademark problems — see below).

- **Won't get dated quickly.** Be careful not to choose names too closely identified with recent trends or that are too limiting. You are likely to change the scope of your products or services over time. Look at all those e-commerce companies that had to drop the words "dot com" from their company names.

- **Conveys the right feeling.** You generally want to choose a name with positive connotations: a day spa named "Haven" or "Oasis" transmits the sense that customers are going to escape the stresses in their lives. "Positive" and "negative," of course, depends a lot on your market. A magazine called *Failure* expected to sell a lot of t-shirts — but only to people under 40, who don't have a problem wearing the word "failure" across their chest.

- **Is easy to spell.** This becomes particularly important when you need customers to remember your Internet domain name or when clients will have to spell your company's name often.

- **Is easy to pronounce.** People have a hard time remembering names they can't say easily. That's why on the back of their chocolate bar wrappers, Ghiradelli printed how to pronounce the name.

- **Is memorable.** This isn't always possible, of course, or even necessary. A company with a straightforward name, "Des Moines Chiropractic Clinic" may develop a better business than a company with a cute name. Names don't determine success.

RED TAPE ALERT!

Before you can make your company a household name, you need to make sure you can use and protect the name. That's where trademark laws come in. With a trademark, you protect yourself from other companies using your name on similar or competing products or services.

The first step in trademarking your name is to do a name search and a trademark search. Use the U.S. Patent and Trademark Office online search (www.uspto.gov — look at searchable databases) and also go to the "whois" section of Network Solutions (www.networksolutions.com). That helps you eliminate a number of names that are already taken. You may want to hire a trademark attorney or search firm to do a more complete search for you.

For more information about trademarks and service marks, turn to page 148 in the chapter on Legal issues.

■ **Is pleasing to the ear.** If you have a sufficient advertising budget, you can make even a "bad" name work. Most of us remember the tagline, "With a name like Smuckers, it has to be good." Again, whether something is pleasing or not has a lot to do with your market. What now seems like an odd choice for a company serving business customers, "Kinko's" was a fine fit when it first opened, serving university students in a beach community.

In the end, however, one of the most important considerations is whether you like the name and feel comfortable with it. After all, you're going to be seeing it and saying it a lot. And don't get hung up trying to decide on your name, slowing down the start of your business. At some point, you just need to make a choice and get on with it.

Use the worksheet on pages 36–37 to compare some of the names you're thinking of for your business, and their pros and cons.

Tagline

Many companies use a motto or tagline either to better explain the nature of the business or to create a feeling about the company or product. A tagline positions your company in the marketplace, and can become the basis of your advertising and marketing pieces.

Some memorable taglines include: Just Do It!™ and You deserve a break today.™

You can use your tagline in TV commercials and on billboards, but it can be just as effective in e-mails, on business cards, or on stationery: "Legal services for the real estate industry," or "Personalized service at practical prices."

Taglines don't have to be "catchy" to be memorable to your target audience. "Manufacturers of custom packing materials for technology products" may seem boring but be very effective if you make and sell boxes for computers. This lets your potential customers know — and reminds current customers — you specialize in exactly what they need.

Some taglines say more than one thing. The tagline of my website, www.RhondaWorks.com, "...for the life of your business" has this aim. I hope users will understand my website is a place to go not only to give a business life, but also to stay throughout the life of their business. And it's also a bit of a pun (since I like puns): "Rhonda works for the life of your business."

You can write down some of your thoughts for taglines and slogans on the "Creating My Identity" worksheet on page 41.

Logo

A logo is an image that can be associated with your company, giving the public another way to remember you. A visual image makes your company more memorable because people learn things and remember things in many different ways — some people are more verbal, some more visual. People use more of their brains, and thus you make more of a mental impact, when they associate you with both words and images.

A good logo conveys something about your company — often a feeling. The Nike "swoosh" shows movement and speed. It's such a strong logo, like McDonald's golden arches, that you don't even need words to know which company is being represented.

My company logo is the Running 'R'.

The Running 'R' was created and designed by graphic designer Jennifer Long of Long Design of Palo Alto, California. She wanted the logo to be associated with me — Rhonda — so the logo implies a face and hair and turns the letter 'R' into a body (in color, the "hair" is yellow — and I'm blonde — so it's really personal). We want to convey that the company helps people move forward, so the logo has movement and energy. And it seems friendly — or at least I think so. I liked the logo so much, I named my publishing company after the logo.

An inexpensive way to create some visual images for your business is to add graphic elements: lines,

BUSINESS NAME COMPARISON CHART

QUESTIONS	NAME	NAME
What are the business names you have considered so far?		
What about the name tells your customers what you do?		
What about the name tells your customers what they get?		
What about the name conveys a feeling? What kind of feeling?		
Are the names already trademarked by another business?		
Are there companies with similar or confusing names?		
Was the name trademarked in a different category? Which one? By whom?		
Who likes the name? Why?		
Who dislikes the name? Why?		
What possible domain name (i.e. web address) would work well with the name?		
Other comments / questions about each name:		

BUSINESS NAME COMPARISON CHART

NAME	NAME	NAME

squares, diamonds. In my first business, I used three sideways triangles to imply movement:

A logo doesn't have to be a drawing or illustration — you can make an "illustration" just of words. This is called a "logotype," and it can be very effective. Think of CocaCola.

Use the "Creating My Identity" worksheet on page 41 to make notes or drawings of possible logos for your business.

If you can afford it, you may want a graphic designer to create your logo. Obviously, when you hire a graphic designer, you should look at their portfolio, see what other companies they have worked for, and look at logos or websites they have designed. But once you've committed yourself to working with a designer, the next step is to help them understand your vision.

Have the designer read your business concept and mission statement you developed on pages 21–22.

Give the designer a sense of your goals and values, so they can consider them in the design. Show them other visual images you like so they can get a sense of your taste and preferences.

Use the guide "Questions to Ask . . . A Graphic Designer" as a starting point. The more information you give your designer to work with, the more quickly, and cost-efficiently, they can develop a logo that works for you.

Colors

Be careful about the choice of colors you use in association with your business. If you use too many colors, it will become expensive to print stationery, business cards, labels, etc. If you use a very trendy color, it can become dated.

Some colors are associated with certain feelings. Blue is considered calming and reassuring, so banks and financial institutions often use blue. Red is considered lucky for some ethnic groups and considered a sign of danger to others. Many colors do not show up well on computers. Check your colors on a

---

QUESTIONS TO ASK . . . A GRAPHIC DESIGNER

- **Ask about:**   Their experience and design process.

    Who's going to do the actual work? They or assistants?

    What fees/costs are involved? What deliverables will you receive for that fee?

- **Ask for:**   At least three to five design options included in initial fee.

    Both black-and-white and color digital versions of your logo, as well as digital templates for all aspects of your identity system you select: business cards, stationery, fax cover sheets, etc.

    Color palette and numbers, both for print and for the Internet.

    A signed agreement giving you ownership and copyright of all designs.

- **Tell them:**   What the company name represents and what your company does.

    Who your target market is: their ages, industries, and concerns.

    What you want your customers to feel about you.

    Whether you want a traditional or more innovative approach.

    What color palettes you like or dislike.

    Who your competitors are and how you're different.

---

number of different computer screens before finalizing your choice.

Since referring to colors just by generic names ("blue," "teal blue," etc.) is very imprecise, professionals have a system by which to identify particular colors. You'll want to learn the "PMS" numbers (which stands for "Pantone Matching System") of the specific color(s) you choose so you can tell future printers and designers the exact colors you want.

Choosing a Domain Name

An important part of choosing a business name and corporate identity today is researching the availability of an appropriate domain name and deciding how much the right domain name is worth to your business.

A "domain name" is the name by which an Internet site is identified and found. It is often referred to, somewhat incorrectly, as your company's "url" or universal resource locator. News reports about companies paying many millions to buy distinctive urls leave the impression a domain name is critical to the success of a business, and it's worth spending a lot of money getting just the right one. But is it?

Most people, and many businesses, get their first url when they sign up for an Internet Service Provider (ISP). So an e-mail address might be something like: johnselectric@aol.com. The advantage to this is that it's easy, and if you use a free ISP (e.g., Juno, Hotmail, Yahoo) it doesn't cost a thing.

Is it better if John gets his own url, so his address might be john@johnselectric.com? Generally, the answer is yes. It seems more businesslike to have your own company domain name. But you'll find most domain names that are natural or obvious for your business have already been taken. This may keep you dragging your feet before putting up a website and getting e-mail. It's much better to get going than to get just the "right" url.

The commonly accepted theory of what makes a good domain name is:

- Seven letters or less
- A real word describing what you sell, or
- Something really catchy.

Remember, a domain name is only as good as the marketing budget — and the business — it's attached to. And the success of your business does not rise or fall on your domain name — no matter how cute, memorable, or descriptive. Most potential customers learn of you through means other than your website: business cards, brochures, networking events. If they like you and your company, they'll type in "hardtorememberurl.com."

I suggest that if you're buying a domain name, don't spend more than the $65 or $70 that www.registrars.com or www.networksolutions.com charges (you can check the availability of website names at those addresses by going to the "Whois" button). Every extra dollar could be spent on your marketing efforts.

Summary

Your start-up phase can be relatively short and inexpensive, especially if you're starting a type of business with low upfront costs, like being an independent consultant. Or, you can have substantial start-up costs, such as renting space, buying equipment, acquiring inventory, and hiring employees.

But one of the most valuable uses of your start-up funds, and one you should not ignore, is a thorough investigation of your company's competitive edge. A catchy name, a memorable logo, or an easy-to-remember domain name can be part of your competitive edge. But many other factors contribute as well, and they are the subject of the next chapter.

WHICH DOMAIN NAMES ARE STILL AVAILABLE?

Use this worksheet to keep track of domain names you've researched. Which domain names are still available from www.networksolutions.com? Which are taken but have owners who could be approached to sell? Which are so similar to the one you've chosen that it's worthwhile to purchase them, too?

Domain Name	Availability?	Owner?	Price?

CREATING MY IDENTITY

Use the space below to begin developing your corporate identity. You may want to draw pictures, as well as use words and phrases, to develop the look, feel, and message you want to convey. You will continue this process in the chapter on Marketing that begins on page 57.

Business Name and Logo

Slogan and Key Words in Marketing Material

Product Design

Packaging

Decor

Style of Clothing Worn by Employees

Other

MY WILD IDEAS FOR GETTING STARTED

my competitive edge

Eugene Kleiner, one of the world's most successful venture capitalists, once told me that most companies don't know what business they're in. By this he meant that most businesspeople don't understand the true basis on which they compete. Yes, they know how to make their products, invent their technologies, but they don't really understand what makes their customers buy from them.

In an increasingly competitive and constantly changing business environment, you need to know more than just HOW to run a business; you need a clear understanding of WHAT business you're really running. You have to understand how you meaningfully differentiate yourself from the competition — your strategic position in the marketplace.

Your company's strategic position can be based on:

- A market niche
- Special features of your product or service
- Quality customer service
- Price
- Convenience, or
- Anything that significantly distinguishes you from others who offer similar services or products.

Of course, the best strategic position is just to be better than the competition — the tennis racket

you've invented plays better, the graphic designs you create are more memorable. But those things are hard to prove. So, how do you develop a clear distinction between yourself and the competition? That is the goal of this chapter.

WHAT BUSINESS AM I IN?

A business relies on more than just a good idea. At some point, real customers will have to decide whether they want to buy your product or service. In the last two chapters, you laid out the beginnings of your business concept. Now you're ready to start on the specifics of building your company.

The single biggest problem facing entrepreneurs is lack of focus. You need to know what pays the bills — what your "bread and butter" business is. When you know how your idea will make money, you will have a "business model."

Rhonda's Rule

focus

Start Your Research by Asking Questions

To develop your business model, you need to do some research — how have other businesses in your industry made money? How much did they make? Who were their customers? What are analysts' expectations for businesses entering this market?

A good way to focus your research efforts is to start by making a general statement that is the basis of your business. For example, if you are planning to start an Internet company providing online psychological therapy, your statement might be: "There is a profitable way to provide psychological counseling via the Internet."

Next, make a list of questions that logically follow from and challenge that statement. Here are some questions you might ask about the online therapy business:

- What companies are already providing such a service?
- What is the size of the market for psychological counseling now?
- What indications are there that consumers would be willing to get counseling on the Internet?
- What portion of the existing psychological counseling market is it reasonable to expect would transfer to online counseling?
- How many consumers who do not currently get counseling could you reasonably expect to be attracted to online counseling?
- What are the key technology issues necessary to conduct such counseling, securely, on the Internet?
- What laws or regulations would affect the ability to offer such services?

Begin your list with the "My Research Questions" worksheet on page 45. Ask yourself tough questions — better to find the answers now rather than after you've invested your time and money. After formulating your list of questions, begin to look for answers. Organize your market research data in the files you set up earlier. Refer to it frequently as you design your marketing plan, look for funding, and launch your operation.

As you prepare your questions, write down where you might be able to find the answers on the worksheet "Research Sources" on page 46. Some high quality sources for market research, such as the Census Bureau and the SEC, are already listed there. Also check www.RhondaWorks.com for other sources of information.

WHO ARE MY CUSTOMERS?

If I asked you to tell me who your customers — or potential customers — are, how would you answer?

Let's say you've created a new breakfast cereal for children: "Yummy Tummy Oats." You've packed "Yummy Tummy Oats" with good things: vitamins, minerals, great nutrition. You figure you're going to wipe out the competition because every parent wants a nutritious breakfast for their child.

There's only one problem: who's your customer? Is it mom or dad pushing the grocery cart down the cereal aisle, comparing the nutrition information on the side of the box?

Or is it the end-user (the "consumer") of your product — the kid — who couldn't care less about nutrition but wants cereal that tastes sweet, has cartoon characters on the package, and toys inside?

Or is it the cereal buyer for the grocery store chain? He couldn't care less about nutrition or cartoon characters. His concerns are more down-to-earth: how much money you're going to spend on advertising, how quickly you replenish inventory, and whether you'll pay him a "stocking fee" to obtain shelf space. Parents and children aren't going to have a chance to buy or eat "Yummy Tummy Oats" if you don't meet the supermarket buyer's needs first.

On top of that, if you don't have your own sales and distribution force, you may first have to find a cereal distributor and convince them to carry your product.

The parent. The child. The store buyer. The distributor. That's a lot of "customers" you have to satisfy

MY RESEARCH QUESTIONS

For each of the following categories, compose a variety of questions you would like to ask for your business. This list of questions will become the basis for your market research. Some categories are discussed in more detail in later chapters, including technology and operations.

Identify Your Industry/Sector: _____

What details and trends do you need to know about your industry/sector?

1. _____

2. _____

Describe Your Products/Services: _____

What details and trends do you need to know about your products/services?

1. _____

2. _____

Describe Your Target Market: _____

What details and trends do you need to know about your target market?

1. _____

2. _____

Identify Your Competition: _____

What details and trends do you need to know about your competition?

1. _____

2. _____

Identify Your Strategic Partners: _____

What details and trends do you need to know about your strategic partners?

1. _____

2. _____

Describe Your Technology: _____

What details and trends do you need to know about your technology?

1. _____

2. _____

Describe Your Operations: _____

What details and trends do you need to know about your operations?

1. _____

2. _____

RESEARCH SOURCES

Type of Information	List Potential Sources	Website/Other Contact Info
U.S. Government	Census Bureau Federal Statistics Online	www.census.gov www.fedstats.gov
State Government	Each state government has a web page	www.state.[two letter state code].us — for example: www.state.ca.us for California www.state.md.us for Maryland
Local/Regional Government	Planning Departments New Business Licenses Regional Planning Associations Chambers of Commerce	
Other Government Info	Government Printing Office Louisiana State University Federal Agencies Directory	www.access.gpo.gov/su_docs www.lib.lsu.edu/gov/fedgov.html
Specific Company Info	Hoover's	www.Hoovers.com
Annual Reports/ SEC filings	Edgar Database	www.sec.gov
Trade Associations	American Society of Association Executives	www.asaenet.org
Other Sources:		
Other Sources:		

with each box of "Yummy Tummy Oats." You give yourself a competitive edge by thinking of each of these "customers." Being responsive to the details that are important to distributors, retailers, sales representatives, etc., helps you plan your marketing materials, operations, packaging, even the nature of the product itself. If yours is an industry where sales reps must purchase their samples, for instance, you can set yourself apart by supplying samples free. If retailers can fit more square packages on a shelf than round packages, you'll be more competitive by choosing a square package.

Even if you think you'll market "directly to consumers" on the Internet, you'll discover there are still many entities between you and your "customer" in cyberspace. In the case of "Yummy Tummy Oats," your intermediary might be the online grocery store, the health food site, or the children's site, but you'll still have more than just parents and kids to please.

As you begin to define your customers, both the end-users and the intermediaries, describe all of the various attributes they have: age, location, industry, purchasing patterns, buying sensitivities, "psychographics" (what motivates them), etc. Be realistic about how people actually behave — not how they should behave.

Use the worksheets on pages 48 and 49 to describe your customers. The first worksheet allows you to

consider the types of "customers" you have. The second worksheet gets you started describing the characteristics of each of those. You may need to make copies of the customer profile worksheet — one for each type of "customer."

Are There Enough Customers?

Okay, so you've defined who your customers are, but are there enough of them? You can't build a successful business — no matter how good your product or service — if there aren't enough customers to sustain you.

The size of the total market may seem an irrelevant factor. Let's say you're planning to start an interior design service in a moderate-size community. You may know there are enough people living in your city to support some interior designers. But look more closely: if your city already has a lot of interior designers, the market may not be big enough to support another. When looking at your customer base, make sure there are enough potential customers for your business to be successful.

If you're looking to find potential investors in your company, particularly venture capitalists or others who hope to gain substantial returns, you'll find they're particularly interested in the size of the total market.

As you compile data on the size of your market, fill in the worksheet below.

SIZE OF MY MARKET

Examine whether the market is large enough to bring you sufficient sales.

Estimated size of my market: _____

   Is this number growing or declining? _____

   By what amount per year? _____

Estimated number of competitors in my market: _____

   Is this number growing or declining? _____

   By what amount per year?_____

Realistic assessment of the opportunity for additional competitors in my market:

   ☐ Outstanding   ☐ Good   ☐ Moderate   ☐ Poor

WHO ARE MY CUSTOMERS?

Describe who your customers are in each of the following categories. You'll find that the number of customers in each category grows the closer you get to the "end user."

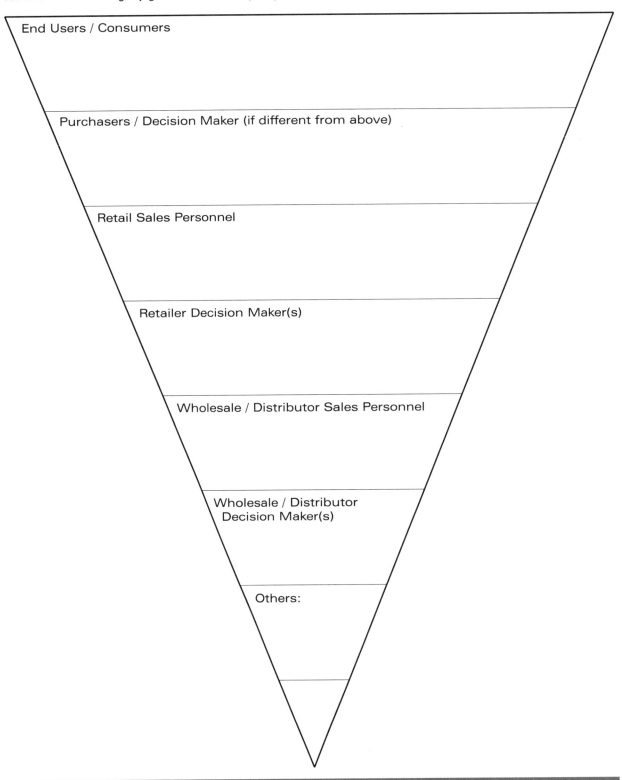

End Users / Consumers

Purchasers / Decision Maker (if different from above)

Retail Sales Personnel

Retailer Decision Maker(s)

Wholesale / Distributor Sales Personnel

Wholesale / Distributor
Decision Maker(s)

Others:

MY CUSTOMER PROFILE

Rank the characteristics of your customers that are most important in determining how receptive they'll be to your product or service. For the characteristics that have no bearing on whether or not they'll buy from you, leave the space blank.

____ Gender   ____ Education level   ____ Children in household

____ Age   ____ Race or Ethnicity   ____ Home ownership

____ Income level   ____ Religious affiliation   ____ Recreational activities

____ Occupation   ____ Marital status   ____ Proximity to your business

Rank the characteristics of your product or service that are most important to your target customers.

____ Price   ____ Convenience   ____ Product Features

____ Service   ____ Reliability   ____ Design

____ Status   ____ Other:_____   ____ Other:_____

Now describe your customers according to the characteristics you have identified. Start with the characteristic you ranked as most important, providing details on how you think that characteristic will influence your customers' buying decisions. You may need to continue this process on a separate sheet, or make copies of this one.

Characteristic #1 _____

Characteristic #2 _____

Characteristic #3 _____

Characteristic #4 _____

Characteristic #5 _____

WHO'S MY COMPETITION?

If I asked you to name your competitors, you're likely to mention the company down the street or across town that sells the same product or service as you. And when I ask you how you're different from your competition, you'll tell me that you're faster, cheaper or better than your cross-town rival. But competition comes in more forms than just the guy down the block. The different types of competitors to keep in mind include:

- **Direct competitors:** These are the companies that you first think of when someone asks, "Who's your competition?" They compete with you directly, selling the same or similar products or services. You may want to dismiss them because you know you are so much better than they are, but customers are likely to compare you to these competitors.

- **Internet-based businesses:** You may be the only company in town that sells purple doorknobs, and in the old days, you could have cornered the local purple doorknob market. Now, customers check the Internet for doorknob suppliers all over the world.

- **Other ways for customers to spend their money:** Customers have lots of ways to spend money. If you sell diamond earrings, a customer may walk out not because they can buy earrings cheaper at another store, but because they decided they'd rather have a vacation or save for their daughter's college education. What makes your product or service more valuable than the other tugs on the pocketbook?

- **Switching Costs and Inertia:** Your biggest competition may be your customers' unwillingness to change. If there is great cost or difficulty switch-ing to you from their current product or service, customers will be unwilling to buy from you even if your product or service is better and cheaper in the long-run. If you're a plumber, someone whose sewer is overflowing has a compelling need. But most customers don't have that type of pressing, pungent need. In most cases, customers have the option not to buy or change at all.

- **Future competitors.** When thinking about your competitors, don't just consider those companies or options that compete with you currently. Who might compete with you in the near future? Once you show you can be successful, who will want to take a piece of that market from you? How can you make it more difficult for them to compete? What are the barriers to entry?

Use the worksheet "My Competitors" on the opposite page to identify and assess your competitors.

WHAT ARE STRATEGIC PARTNERS?

You don't have to do everything alone. A strategic partnership is a relationship with another company for purposes such as distribution, product development, promotion, or add-on sales. A strong strategic partner that is already serving your target market can give you a real edge in reaching that market.

For example, you might use a partnership for:

- **Distribution Agreement.** This is an agreement whereby one company carries another's product line and sells its products or services.

- **Licensing.** One company may grant permission to another to use its product, name, or trademark. Instead of selling your product or service directly, you might license it to another company to sell under its name.

- **Cooperative Advertising**. This type of advertising occurs when two companies are mentioned in an advertisement and each company pays part of the costs. This is a frequent practice in many industries.

Rhonda's Rule

customers do what they want or need to do, not what they should do.

MY COMPETITORS

Use this worksheet to identify your competitors. What businesses compete with you directly? What other forces influence how or if your customers will spend their money on your product or service? Be realistic and honest in this assessment — it will help you build a better business and give you a competitive edge.

Competitor	Their Advantages/Strengths	My Advantages/Strengths
Direct Competitors:		
Internet Based Competitors:		
Other Ways to Spend Money:		
Inertia Factors:		
Potential Future Competitors:		

POTENTIAL STRATEGIC PARTNERS

Use this space to start a list of potential strategic partners, how you can help each other, and how you can secure a relationship with them.

Potential Strategic Partners	Mutual Benefits	Ways to Start a Relationship

- **Bundling.** This is a relationship between two companies where one company includes another company's product or service as part of a total package. You keep your own identity, but get the advantage of being included in their package.

Securing a major company as a key partner can not only give your company specific competitive advantages, but also credibility with customers and funders.

Use the worksheet "Potential Strategic Partners" on page 52 to identify those with whom you might form a partnership in which you both benefit.

WHAT ARE MY MILESTONES?

You gain a competitive edge by setting and reaching specific goals. Identifying particular milestones, with target dates, gives you and others a way to judge how much — and how fast — you are making progress in building your company.

When you're in the midst of building a company, and there are so many things on your "To Do" list, you may feel like you're making no progress whatso-

---

Rhonda's Rule

things take longer and cost more than planned

---

ever. Having a milestone list that you can refer to, showing the things you've already accomplished, will remind you that you are, indeed, moving toward your goals.

Use the two worksheets on Milestones — Achieved to Date and those you hope to achieve in the future, on pages 54 and 55 — to keep track of your progress.

Summary

Today, defining a strategic position is as important for the proverbial "mom and pop" small business as it is for a high technology company. It's not enough to hang out a shingle that says, "I sell shoes," or "I sell e-commerce technology." You have to have something that's unique, that few others can offer, that makes your customers want to buy from you. The more you understand about your own company — and how you differ from the competition — the better able you are to compete.

MY MILESTONES ACHIEVED TO DATE

State the specific objectives you have achieved and when you achieved each one.

Event	Specifics	Date Completed
Incorporation		
Lease Signed		
Key Employees Hired:		
Initial Financing Secured		
Product Design Completed		
Market Testing Completed		
Trademarks / Patents Secured		
Strategic Partnerships Secured		
First Product Shipped		
Level of Sales Reached ($)		
Level of Sales Reached (units)		
Level of Employees Reached		
Profit Level Reached		
Second Product Line Developed		
Second Product Line Tested		
Second Product Line Shipped		
Additional Financing Secured		
Debts Retired		
Additional Location Opened		
Website Launched		
Other:		

MY FUTURE MILESTONES

State your specific future objectives and when you plan to achieve each one.

Event	Specifics	Goal Date
Incorporation		
Lease Signed		
Key Employees Hired:		
Initial Financing Secured		
Product Design Completed		
Market Testing Completed		
Trademarks / Patents Secured		
Strategic Partnerships Secured		
First Product Shipped		
Level of Sales Reached ($)		
Level of Sales Reached (units)		
Level of Employees Reached		
Profit Level Reached		
Second Product Line Developed		
Second Product Line Tested		
Second Product Line Shipped		
Additional Financing Secured		
Debts Retired		
Additional Location Opened		
Website Launched		
Other:		

MY WILD IDEAS FOR MY COMPETITIVE EDGE

marketing, networking, & sales

You have to have customers to stay in business: it's the most basic business truth. That's why an effective marketing plan to communicate with, motivate, and secure customers is vital for your company's success. Since reaching customers costs money, and money is always limited, your marketing strategy must be carefully and thoughtfully designed.

First, let's understand our terms: Marketing is designed to increase customer awareness and deliver your message. It includes activities such as advertising, creating brochures and collateral materials, and public relations.

Marketing also includes what's called "networking," meeting potential customers and referral sources through informal activities, such as joining organizations, attending industry events, or taking people to lunch. In smaller companies, networking may be the major marketing activity.

Sales, on the other hand, is the direct action taken to secure customer orders. Sales encompasses telemarketing, sales calls, special promotions, and direct-mail solicitations.

In all of these activities, whether it's a direct sales call, an advertising campaign, or a Rotary luncheon, you are conveying a message about your business, and more importantly, what your product or service does for your customer — its features and benefits.

In this chapter, you will design and plan a marketing and sales strategy, centered around your message.

WHAT'S MY COMPANY'S MESSAGE?

In the last two chapters, you began developing your company's identity and strategic position. These first steps are vital to your company's image and position in the marketplace, and you'll refer to them frequently in this chapter. Now, you've got to take that information to the next level — building an actual marketing program.

Every business sends a message in its marketing. Your message is based on the strategic position your company stakes out for itself, such as "low-price leader" or "one-day service." The message also exploits a market niche: "specialists in estate planning" or "software for architects."

Most marketing strategists agree that people buy benefits, not features. Customers are more concerned about how a purchase will affect their lives than about how the company achieves those results. So your marketing message must tell customers what they get, rather than just the detailed specifics of what your product or service does.

Rhonda's Rule

tell people what they get, not what you do

The Four P's of Marketing

What messages do you give customers to motivate them to purchase your product or service? Traditional marketing experts emphasize the elements known as "the Four P's," in influencing customers to buy.

1. **Product.** The tangible product or service itself.
2. **Price.** The cost advantage.
3. **Place.** The location's convenience and decor.
4. **Promotion.** The amount and nature of the marketing activities.

These elements leave a lot out of the marketing picture, however, especially as customers look for products or services not just to fill an immediate need but to enhance their overall sense of well-being.

What Customers Want: Rhonda's Five F's

A more effective way to sum up what customers want is through the Five F's:

1. **Functions.** How does the product or service meet customers' concrete needs?
2. **Finances.** How will the purchase affect their overall financial situation, not just the price of the product or service, but other savings and increased productivity?
3. **Freedom.** How convenient is it to purchase and use the product or service? How will they gain more time and less worry in other aspects of their lives?
4. **Feelings.** How does the product or service make customers feel about themselves, and how does it affect and relate to their self-image? Do they like and respect the salesperson and the company?
5. **Future.** How will they deal with the product or service and company over time? Will support and service be available? How will the product or service affect their lives in the coming years, and will they have an increased sense of security about the future?

Customers, of course, want to receive benefits in all these areas, and you should be aware of how your product or service fulfills the entire range of their needs. However, your primary message must concentrate on one or two of these benefits that most effectively motivates your customers.

The worksheet "My Company's Message" on page 59 helps you plan how to convey your message to your customers.

The Elevator Pitch

When someone asks, "What does your company do?" you need a short, clear answer that quickly sums up the nature of your business. This has to be short! Here's the test for whether a marketing statement is brief enough: could you explain your business if you ran into a potential client on an elevator ride in a three story building? That's why it's called the "elevator pitch." If it takes you more than three floors to describe your company, you're saying too much.

The message must not only be short; it must be clear. Unless you're in a highly technical field, your neighbor or your grandmother should be able to understand your services well enough to describe them to someone else. After all, you want other people to be out there marketing for you, too, don't you? If people you meet can't quickly understand and grasp the nature of your company's offerings, they'll never be able to send business your way.

Your elevator pitch should touch — very briefly — on the products or services you sell, what market you serve, and your competitive advantage. If you're in an easy-to-understand business, your elevator pitch theoretically could be very short: "I sell real estate." But that wouldn't distinguish you from the thousands of other realtors out there. A more memorable elevator pitch gives listeners a reason to remember you: "I sell homes in the North County area, specializing in first-time buyers."

The worksheet on page 60 will help you develop your elevator pitch. After you've written a draft or two, time yourself saying it out loud. Can you deliver it in three floors or less? If not, you've said too much.

MY COMPANY'S MESSAGE

Keeping the Five F's in mind, describe the message you are trying to convey to customers about your product or service.

Functions:

Finances:

Freedom:

Feelings:

Future:

Which of these messages is the most important in motivating your target market to purchase?

MY ELEVATOR PITCH

Use this worksheet to develop your elevator pitch. Remember to keep it short; focus on what customers get, not what you do; and make it easy to remember.

My Company...

Named:
Does:
Serves Which Market:
Makes Money By:
Is Like What Other Companies:
Will Succeed Because It:
Aims to Achieve:

HOW DO I CREATE MY MARKETING PROGRAM?

Once you have clarified what you want to tell customers, you have to get the message out there. How will you reach your customers? The methods you choose are called your "marketing vehicles."

You have a variety of marketing vehicles to choose from. The best method(s) for you depends on your marketing budget, target market, product or service, and marketing message.

Create a Marketing Budget!

The most important part of your marketing program is that you can afford it. Every marketing vehicle costs money, so carefully plan how you intend to spend your marketing dollars. Often the best marketing vehicles are not the most obvious or the most expensive. A large ad in a specialty publication may prove far more effective and less expensive than a small one in a general newspaper.

If you spend a ton of money on a huge advertising campaign but it leaves you without the money to pay the rent or make payroll, you're going to be in hot water. So, as you develop your marketing plan, refer to your overall budget in the Money chapter. Make sure you can afford the choices you make.

Choosing a Marketing Mix

In devising your overall marketing program, be sure you look for:

- **Fit.** Your marketing vehicles must reach your actual target customer and be appropriate to your image.
- **Mix.** Use more than one method so customers get exposure to you from a number of sources.
- **Repetition.** It takes many exposures before a customer becomes aware of a message.
- **Affordability.**

The many worksheets on the following pages will help you choose between a variety of marketing vehicles. Several worksheets focus on specific marketing vehicles, such as printed materials, trade shows, and public relations. The worksheet "Marketing Vehicle Comparison Chart," helps turn your message into a comprehensive marketing program using the following techniques for getting your message to the people you most want to reach:

- **Printed Marketing Material.** Every company needs "stuff" to hand out. Whether you call them brochures, collateral sales material, or "leave behinds," you have to have printed materials. Even in this day of websites and e-mails, you'll need words printed on paper. The most important piece of printed material is your business card. Get those

WHAT WOULD RHONDA DO . . . FOR BUSINESS CARDS

We made all our first RhondaWorks business cards at Kinko's, but you could do this at any decent copy shop with color digital printers.

First, we laid out a template for our business card. Check with your copy shop for the format they want — usually "10 up" or ten cards to a page, with "crop marks."

Next, we e-mailed the computer file of the business cards to Kinko's, selected the very best card stock they had, and had them produce the cards on a digital color printer — not a copier. That way each page was an "original."

At the time, we paid a $10 set-up fee, a $9 card cutting fee (don't do this yourself; it looks messy) and $1 per page print fee. We printed 10 pages, with 10 cards per page. The 100 four-color cards totaled only $29, and took less than an hour. If you don't need a lot of cards, you don't have to use the whole 10 for the same employee, so one employee could have 50 cards and two others could have 20 and 30, all for the same $29!

done right away. Use the worksheet "My Printing Needs" below to plan and budget your printed materials.

- **Customer-Based Marketing.** The best business is repeat business. So remind past customers you exist. Keep a mailing list, send postcards or e-mail when you have special offers, write a newsletter, or just send a note or holiday greeting. Contact past customers no less than twice a year and no more than every other month. Specialty items, such as pens, mugs, or calendars, are another good way to remind customers you exist. And most importantly, don't be afraid to ask customers for referrals!

- **Trade Shows.** Trade shows are a great way to meet potential new customers and for them to meet you. A face-to-face meeting makes doing business with you a lot more inviting, and the trade show setting makes it comfortable for them to ask you questions about your company. Trade shows can be expensive — the cost of being an exhibitor, preparing your booth, printing marketing materials, and, of course, bringing enough personnel to staff

> ## Rhonda's Rule
> **people do business with people they like, so get to know your customers as people**

the booth. But a trade show is often the best place to reach your target market. Before choosing to exhibit, however, find out as much as you can from the show's organizers about who will be attending. Talk to exhibitors from previous years' shows to see how successful they were. Use the worksheet "Trade Shows and Industry Events" to keep a list of potential trade shows to attend or exhibit at.

- **Public Relations/Publicity.** The best publicity is often "free" publicity. Getting a story about your business in the local newspaper or on TV can be more powerful than a paid advertisement. But that's not to say that such coverage won't cost you: while you don't pay for the stories directly, you may have to hire a public relations specialist, because

MY PRINTING NEEDS

What do you need printed professionally? What requires color? Use this worksheet to project how many printed materials you will need.

	Color or B&W?	How Many Needed?	Printer	Cost per Unit	Total Cost
☐ Business cards					
☐ Brochures					
☐ Pamphlets					
☐ Fliers					
☐ Publicity photo					
☐ Advertising specialties (mugs, pens, etc.)					
☐ Signage					
☐ Vehicle signage					
☐ Uniforms, t-shirts, etc.					
☐ Other:					

TRADE SHOWS AND INDUSTRY EVENTS

Use this worksheet to keep track of trade shows or events that you should consider attending. Under "Costs" list both the cost to attend or to exhibit and "early-bird registration." Under "Attendees" list as much specific detail about the type of people who attend as possible. If you enter your "Deadlines" at www.RhondaWorks.com, Rhonda will send you a reminder.

Name of Show/Event: _____

Sponsor: _____   Date: _____

Location: _____   Costs: _____

_____   Attendees: _____

Deadlines: _____   _____

Notes: _____

_____

Name of Show/Event: _____

Sponsor: _____   Date: _____

Location: _____   Costs: _____

_____   Attendees: _____

Deadlines: _____   _____

Notes: _____

_____

Name of Show/Event: _____

Sponsor: _____   Date: _____

Location: _____   Costs: _____

_____   Attendees: _____

Deadlines: _____   _____

Notes: _____

_____

Name of Show/Event: _____

Sponsor: _____   Date: _____

Location: _____   Costs: _____

_____   Attendees: _____

Deadlines: _____   _____

Notes: _____

_____

GETTING PUBLICITY

Use this worksheet to list ideas and issues related to you and your business that can generate news stories or other free publicity for your company.

Timely Stories: Tie your activities to events that generate their own publicity, such as holidays, local celebrations, or new legislation.

Creative Angles: The unusual, amusing, or extraordinary always gets attention. If you can, involve celebrities.

Joint Publicity Opportunities: Leverage the power of other organizations to gain visibility; consider unlikely coalitions, not just similar interest groups.

Visual Stories: Television, in particular, needs visually stimulating stories, but newspapers also use visually interesting photos. Avoid "BOPSA:" Bunch of People Sitting Around.

Issues on which You're the "Expert": Reporters need reliable sources they can turn to quickly. Provide trustworthy, objective information, preferably with statistics.

GETTING PUBLICITY

Media Contacts:

Keep a list of potential media contacts: reporters, editors, columnists who cover issues/stories relating to your company

Name: _____   Name: _____

Title: _____   Title: _____

Media Outlet: _____   Media Outlet: _____

Areas of Interest: _____   Areas of Interest: _____

Contact Info: _____   Contact Info: _____

_____   _____

Name: _____   Name: _____

Title: _____   Title: _____

Media Outlet: _____   Media Outlet: _____

Areas of Interest: _____   Areas of Interest: _____

Contact Info: _____   Contact Info: _____

_____   _____

Name: _____   Name: _____

Title: _____   Title: _____

Media Outlet: _____   Media Outlet: _____

Areas of Interest: _____   Areas of Interest: _____

Contact Info: _____   Contact Info: _____

_____   _____

Name: _____   Name: _____

Title: _____   Title: _____

Media Outlet: _____   Media Outlet: _____

Areas of Interest: _____   Areas of Interest: _____

Contact Info: _____   Contact Info: _____

_____   _____

MARKETING VEHICLES COMPARISON CHART

QUESTIONS	DIRECT MAIL BROCHURES, FLIERS, COUPONS	SIGNAGE/ DISPLAYS VEHICLE/BUILDING SIGNAGE, BILLBOARDS	PRINT MEDIA NEWSPAPERS, MAGAZINES, SPECIALTY PUBLICATIONS
What market do they reach?			
How big is their reach?			
What percentage of their market is my target market?			
What is the Cost per Thousand (CPM) reached?			
What frequency will I need to be effective?			
What is the reasonable immediate response I can expect?			
How expensive is the ad to prepare?			
What are this vehicle's advantages?			
What are this vehicle's disadvantages?			
Other:			

MARKETING VEHICLES COMPARISON CHART

BROADCAST MEDIA TELEVISION, RADIO	ONLINE WEBSITE DESIGN, HOSTING, ADVERTISING	PHONE DIRECTORIES YELLOW PAGES, OR OTHER DIRECTORIES	TRADE SHOWS	PUBLIC RELATIONS, PUBLICITY

good publicity is usually the result of an ongoing public relations program. Do your homework. Get to know which media outlets (TV, radio, newspapers, Internet sites, trade publications) cover the type of stories you might have. Of course, you need a story that readers, listeners, or viewers will find interesting, a "hook" or angle that makes your story informative, amusing, or timely. Use the "Getting Publicity" worksheets on pages 64–65 to keep a list of publicity opportunities and potential media contacts.

- **Advertising.** Advertising works. It gets your company's name and message to a large number of people with relatively little work on your part. But it costs money. Don't buy ads based merely on the number of people they'll reach; make sure the ad is reaching the right people: the customers you want. A badly designed and written ad may be worse than no ad at all, so spend the time and money to develop a good one. Run ads repetitively; professionals estimate it takes nine exposures to an ad before someone even notices it.

- **Networking.** Join professional organizations. Participate in community groups. Ask for referrals. Networking is a vital part of a company's marketing program. It's so important, especially for a small business, that a larger section of this chapter is devoted to it.

- **Your Website.** You'll have many purposes for your company's website, so I've addressed the issue of designing, managing, and using your website in the chapter, "Technology and Communication." But certainly your website is a key part of your marketing program. Your customers and potential customers will turn to it first to get information about you and your company. Always keep your website in mind as you develop and grow your marketing activities.

- **"Guerrilla Marketing."** This is a very inexact term that's come to mean off-beat, unusual marketing techniques. It could be inexpensive (putting up notices on bulletin boards in Laundromats) or very expensive (flying a blimp over a professional football game). Because customers are constantly bombarded with advertising messages, the more

creative you are in your advertising and promotion, the more likely you are to get noticed.

For more information on how to develop and implement a marketing program, or for marketing vehicles specific to your industry or region of the country, visit www.RhondaWorks.com.

And don't forget to design your marketing program with your budget in mind. If you don't have the money for an ad campaign now, you may have it someday. Until then, shake hands, "do" lunch, and network . . .

NETWORK, NETWORK NETWORK!

When you want an accountant or architect, a plumber or painter, you probably ask a friend or fellow entrepreneur for a name. When you're the business, rather than the customer, you want to be at the tip of someone's tongue when they're asked that question. It's the oldest, and probably most effective marketing technique: "word-of-mouth advertising."

All types of businesses depend on referrals. Unfortunately for a start-up business, the best way to get referrals is to run a terrific business for many, many years. What do you do in the meantime? Here are a few techniques that can speed up the process and increase the number of people who'll remember your name the next time someone asks them for a referral:

Participate in professional organizations.
Professional or industry colleagues are a major source of referrals, and if you don't belong to an industry or trade group, you're missing opportunities. My friend, Jennifer, is a health care marketing specialist who doesn't even have her phone number

Rhonda's Rule
carry your business card with you

ORGANIZATIONS TO JOIN

Research the best organizations or associations to join. These may be related to your industry or your locality. Consider whether it charges a membership fee and how it can help you grow your business.

Organization	Membership Fees and Duration	Activities, Events, Classes or Services Offered	How Will it Help my Business?

NETWORKING CONTACTS

Use this form to keep track of people you contact or want to contact to build your business. Also enter follow-up dates at www.RhondaWorks.com.

Contact Company Name Address City, State, Zip	Phone & E-mail	Last time Contacted	What You Discussed / Referrals Obtained	Follow-up Date and/or Thank-you Sent

listed — she gets all her work through referrals. Jennifer was president of a health care marketing group and belongs to a number of other professional organizations. People in the field know and respect her, and she's got more work than she can handle.

Get active in community groups. Helping your community is not just good citizenship, it's good business. People who've met you at a bake sale for the Girl Scouts or saw your company's name listed as a sponsor of the Earth Day Walk-a-Thon are more likely to do business with you. If there is a cause or organization that you're particularly interested in, get VERY involved. Other supporters are likely to be very loyal to your business.

Do EXCEPTIONAL work. When you do something that not only satisfies a customer but delights and surprises them, they'll remember it. If a car repair shop washes your car before returning it or a butcher adds a bone for your dog, you're not only going to come back, you're going to tell your friends. And you'll be part of their "word-of-mouth" advertising campaign.

A Word About Your "Grand Opening"

If you're just starting your business — or expanding — a good way to let people know you exist is to hold a "Grand Opening." This isn't just for retail

---

WHAT WOULD RHONDA DO... AT A BUSINESS LUNCH

Most inexperienced lunchers believe the main purpose of a business lunch is either to: a) conduct business, or b) eat lunch, and they're unsure how to mix the two. Don't worry! Business lunches aren't about either business or lunch; they're about building relationships. Here are the keys to a successful business lunch:

Listen. Listen to what the other person cares about, what makes him or her tick. Ask questions. You don't want to conduct an interview, but you'd be surprised how smart people think you are if you ask questions and listen to their replies. You'll learn how to relate to the other person better as you go forward in a business setting.

Go for no reason. Don't make the lunch seem like a sales call. Instead, ask for an informal get-together: "We've been doing business together for almost a year. I'd like to take you to lunch and get to know you a little better." Or, be a little less straightforward, "I'm often in your area, how about having lunch sometime?"

Order slow food. Preferably, have the other person suggest a place to eat. If you have a limited budget, you choose a nice, mid-priced restaurant. Forget McDonald's. Don't be in a rush. Order "slow food," not "fast food." You want as much time with your guest as possible.

Don't order messy food! Pass on the spaghetti, and be careful about piling chili on the burger. Forget the 'three-martini' business lunch. It's wisest not to drink any alcoholic beverage at lunch, and only do so if your companion is also. No matter what your companion does, stick to an absolute one-drink limit. This, after all, is still business.

Turn off your cell phone. Stay focused on your companion. Remember, your goal is to listen and learn.

Bring your credit card or sufficient cash. If you did the inviting, pick up the tab, even if your guest says, "I can put this on my company's credit card." But don't have a scene arguing over the check. You can just say, "You can get the next one." Some companies have policies that don't permit employees to be treated; in that case, split the tab.

Good luck and bon appetit!

RED TAPE ALERT!

Beware! Not all marketing expenses are treated the same by the IRS. While taking an ad out in a newspaper is 100% deductible, taking a client out to lunch is not. Although business entertainment is often the major marketing expense for smaller companies, most meal and entertainment expenses are only 50% deductible.

For example, if you spend $60 on lunch for you and your customer, you can only claim $30 as a deductible expense. Meals are also only 50% deductible when you're traveling, even on a totally business-related trip. There are a very few exceptions to the 50% rule, such as when you're providing food for a company employee retreat or picnic. But far more often, the IRS takes a careful and dim view of entertainment expenses. Be able to verify that business was actually discussed and you had a legitimate business purpose.

businesses. You can hold an "Open House" at your new office space, a "Launch Party" even for a home-based or virtual business (have it at a restaurant or other rented or borrowed space) or a "Product Launch" event for a new product or service.

You don't have to hold such an event on your first day, week, or even month in business. Give yourself a little time to get your business underway. Think of this as a marketing event — not just a celebration. Draw up an invitation list of all those you want to know about your business, even if you know they won't attend the party. This can include potential customers, suppliers, friends, business reporters, trade association or community organization leaders. Send a nice invitation or announcement and perhaps issue a press release. Put yourself on the map!

HOW DO I GET CUSTOMERS TO BUY?

If your marketing campaign is successful, you'll soon be having prospects interested in your product or service. Now you have to make the actual sale.

Getting Your First Customer

While the Starship Enterprise may go "where no one else has gone before," most customers only follow where others lead. Customers like to patronize companies and purchase products that others have already chosen. What a dilemma: you have to have

customers to get customers. But don't despair; there are a number of tricks to snare that first one.

The simplest is to give your product or service away. This isn't as stupid as it sounds. Technology companies often give potential customers "beta" or test versions of their software. They use this as a way both to improve their product and to expose future buyers to what they make.

Another approach is to charge your early clients far less than they would be able to get elsewhere and less than you're likely to charge later. This "introductory pricing" approach is very effective.

Another way to find your first customer is to ask your competitors for excess work they can't handle. Yes, I said "competitors." One of the biggest mistakes I made when I started was that I avoided talking to others in my field. I figured they would view me as a threat, and the less they knew about me, the better. I was wrong. It turned out my "competitors" were a great source both for new business and industry information. Competitors may be interested in subcontracting or referring work to you.

If you can do so legally, or if you're on good terms with your former employer, see if there are customers you can take from your last job. Some of the most successful small businesses are those set up to serve customers or offer the product lines that bigger businesses can no longer handle profitably.

A final word of warning: if you're making a major switch of career, don't expect your friends, family, or former colleagues to be eager to be your first customers. These are folks who've thought of you in one context for a long time, and it's going to take a while before they'll see you in a new light. So get out there and market to strangers.

Your Sales Pitch

Most people wrongly believe a good salesperson is someone who can talk well. That's only half of it. It's equally important to be able to listen well. By listening to customers, you find out which issues are most important to them in making a purchasing decision.

At some point, though, you will need to make the pitch — actually ask a "prospect," a prospective customer, to buy your product or service. A sales pitch can come in many forms, but it has three distinct stages:

- Your pitch
- The customer's concerns and objections
- Your rejoinder, or reply, to those concerns and objections

After you've been in business for a while, you'll know the objections or concerns that keep most prospects from making the decision to buy. Work on those, so you sound confident in responding to them should they arise in the course of a sales call.

It's generally best to anticipate objections and respond to them before they're even raised. This way, you can address whatever shortcomings or problems the prospect may be thinking about but doesn't want to mention out loud.

Use the worksheet "My Sales Pitch" on page 74 to outline the points you'll make to prospective customers and how you'll handle their reservations and objections.

Looking for Leads

Before you can make your sales pitch, you have to find prospective customers to pitch to. A potential customer is referred to as a "sales lead."

Your sales leads are a natural outgrowth of defining your target market. The better you've defined your target, the easier it will be for you to focus in on your most likely prospects. If you manufacture plumbing fixtures, for instance, you will have more effective sales efforts if you know whether your primary sales target is new construction or remodels, residential or commercial, contractors or home-improvement consumers.

Most smaller and newer companies get their first sales leads through joining industry, entrepreneur, or community groups. Trade and industry associations are a particularly good way to find prospective customers, and often, they will sell or rent their membership lists. One benefit of exhibiting at tradeshows is that you often receive a list of attendees, and that can be a good basis for sales leads. Joining the Chamber of Commerce often gives you a list of other local Chamber members.

If you are in the business-to-business (b-to-b) market rather than the business-to-consumer (b-to-c) market, it can be easier to find names of companies you want to target. If you are very clear on your criteria, you can compile your own list from the phone directory or from the Internet. You can also buy lists from list brokers and companies such as Dun & Bradstreet. Use the worksheet on page 75 to get started.

Finding the right person in any company is always a challenge, however, no matter how good a list you put together. Good leads are worth a lot!

Summary

You've got to have customers. To get customers, you have to let people know about your products and services. You do that through marketing, networking, and sales. Be certain your marketing program is affordable. Often less expensive, more targeted activities bring greater success than expensive advertising campaigns. Join trade associations, stay in touch with referral sources, and take your good customers to lunch.

MY SALES PITCH

Use this worksheet to develop your sales pitch. Know your strengths and be able to explain those quickly. Under "My Pitch," list your key strengths that distinguish you from your competition. Then, anticipate objections prospective customers might raise under "Their Objections." Finally, prepare a "Rejoinder" that counters the objection and convinces your prospect to buy.

MY PITCH	THEIR OBJECTIONS	REJOINDER

SOURCES OF SALES LEADS

You have many ways for finding potential customers. One of the best ways is to network through trade associations, strategic partners, and other organizations and companies in your industry. You can also buy lists from list brokers for your direct marketing efforts. Use this worksheet to list these various sources of sales leads.

	Name/Contact Information	Number and Type of Prospects	Cost	Notes
Trade Associations: _____ _____ _____ _____				
List Brokers: _____ _____ _____ _____				
Strategic Partners: _____ _____ _____ _____				
Other Organizations: _____ _____ _____ _____				
Other Companies: _____ _____ _____ _____				

MY WILD IDEAS

Wild Ideas for Marketing:

Wild Ideas for Networking:

Wild Ideas for Sales:

people

People are your most important resource. No matter how great your business concept or technology, without great employees, your business will not succeed.

This is particularly true in a growing business because you have so much to do: develop new strategies, create new alliances, plan new operations, and secure additional sales. These activities place the greatest demands on you and your people.

ME: HOW DO I MANAGE MYSELF?

The first person you have to manage, train, and motivate is yourself. Investing in your continual growth and well-being is a business necessity, not a luxury.

Getting Smarter

Making your employees more knowledgeable and more skilled is a good investment. The more competent each employee is, the more valuable they are to the company. The same is true with you, too. You need to sharpen your skills and increase your knowledge continually. Do something at least once a year to upgrade your abilities.

- **Credentials and Certification:** Many professions and businesses require some form of certification just to open up shop. You can't be a doctor or lawyer, a hairdresser or realtor, without proper credentials. Even when not required, additional certification can set you apart from the competition, enabling you to command higher fees and gain market share. Industry associations are good sources of information about certification and credential programs.

- **Classes and Seminars:** Even when you don't have time for a complete course of study, short classes or seminars can improve your knowledge and skills. Such programs are offered by trade associations (often at the same time as trade shows), community colleges and university extension programs, entrepreneurs' and other business organizations, computer learning centers, as well as for-profit seminar programs.

- **Trade Shows/Conventions:** These are quick and easy ways to catch up on new developments in your industry, identify new competitors, better understand customers, and get re-motivated.

- **"Play around" with new technology:** Even if you don't like taking classes, you can increase your technical skills by buying new software or equipment, a training manual, and teaching yourself.

- **Surf the web:** The Internet is the world's biggest encyclopedia. If you don't have time to take seminars or attend trade shows, the Internet is always available. Find a topic you'd like to learn more about (marketing, human resources, business planning) and start searching.

- **Read:** The fastest, cheapest, most effective way to learn things is to read. Become a regular reader of business and trade publications, your local newspaper, Internet sites, business books.

Use the worksheet Getting Smarter on page 79 for listing classes and opportunities for improving your skill set.

Getting Focused

There aren't enough hours in the day to do all the things you need to do, so you need to maximize your time. For most people that means getting focused.

- **Make a list:** Use the checklist in this book or at www.RhondaWorks.com as the basis for your personal "To Do" list. A daily list enables you to better manage and remember all the things you have to do. If you use the "To Do" list at www.RhondaWorks.com, I'll send you e-mail reminders of your priorities.

- **Make things routine:** Parts of every business are repeated over and over. Make a computer file called "templates" with your standard documents: proposals, letters, invoices, description of your services or company, etc.

- **Do the most important things early in the day:** Emergencies come up. Calls or meetings take longer than planned. Take care of those "must do" items at the start of your workday.

- **Turn off the phone:** Wean yourself from the need to answer every phone call. Let an assistant or voice mail pick up.

Setting Goals

Yogi Berra once said, "If you don't know where you're going, you will wind up somewhere else." Your goals are a guide for your business journey.

Since most goals seem overwhelming ("Be financially secure within 10 years"), you have to break them down into far more manageable tasks:

- Make your goals well-defined, quantifiable, and time-specific: "For the next three months, I'll call five new prospects a week."
- Translate those goals into short-term objectives: "I'll call three prospects on Monday and two on Tuesday."
- Put the most emphasis on goals within your control rather than those determined by others — "I'll make 8 cold calls this week" instead of "I'll get 3 new customers."
- Be realistic given the many demands on you.

Since some goals are outside your complete control ("I will increase sales by 25%"), give yourself a deadline on how long you'll focus on those goals before moving on. Use the "Goals" worksheets on pages 6–7 to outline your goals and when you hope to achieve them.

My Health

If you bought an expensive piece of equipment for your business, you'd maintain and take care of it. But we often neglect the most important, valuable asset our company has: our own body.

Taking care of one's own health sometimes seems self-indulgent: going to the gym or sitting down to eat a healthy lunch feels like a waste of time when you could be at your desk, making sales calls, and eating fast food.

Your physical well-being is an important corporate asset, regardless of your line of work. If you neglect it, you'll lower the value of your assets, not to mention reduce both the lifespan of your resource and its productivity.

Taking care of your emotional well-being is also part of taking care of your health. Maintain relationships, friendships, and family commitments. Single-minded people not only lose perspective of what's important, but over time are less able to deal with others and grow to resent work.

Finally, take time each and every day to appreciate someone or something. Admire the scenery, laugh at a joke, play with a child, listen to a friend. You'll be

GETTING SMARTER

List ways to continually improve your knowledge and skills.

Credentials/Certification to get:

Topics of Interest to Pursue:

Publications/Books to Read:

Internet Sites to Visit:

Classes, Workshops, Trade Shows, Speeches To Attend:

If you enter the dates below in your "To Do" List at www.RhondaWorks.com, Rhonda will send you a reminder:

Name of Event/Speaker:

Last Day for Early Registration:

Sponsoring Organization:

Last Day to Register:

Date(s) Held:

Cost:

Time:

Discounts?

Location:

Name of Event/Speaker:

Last Day for Early Registration:

Sponsoring Organization:

Last Day to Register:

Date(s) Held:

Cost:

Time:

Discounts?

Location:

surprised at how much more you enjoy your work if you enjoy your life.

My Support System

Building a company can be lonely work. Advisors can be one of the most valuable assets an entrepreneur can have, providing support, contacts, and advice. Even if yours is a one-person business, you'll want people you can turn to for guidance as you start, run, and grow your company.

Business Buddies/Mentors: In my early years, I had what I call a "business buddy," Jennifer Arthur. Jennifer was a good friend who had started a consulting practice at about the same time that I did. Jennifer and I would share proposal templates, billing and pricing advice, solutions to problems with clients, sometimes just a conversation in the middle of the afternoon when we felt overwhelmed or lonely. Finding someone who's in a similar stage of development as you can be a great way to think through ideas and learn from one another.

If you can find a more experienced businessperson, you might be able to secure an informal "mentor." Many accomplished entrepreneurs enjoy helping others build their businesses.

Don't be afraid to ask for help. Many people are willing to be of assistance if you're capable, professional, and realistic about what kind of help you need and they're able to offer.

Entrepreneurs' Groups: There's been an explosion of organizations serving entrepreneurs in local communities. These groups typically have regular meetings with guest speakers — experts in management, technology, financing, etc. They also provide networking opportunities to meet potential customers, suppliers, and "business buddies." Some organizations are formed around industries, others around stages of business development, or gender or ethnic groups.

Board of Directors: This is typically a legal entity required for an incorporated company. (Check with a lawyer for rules relating to corporations and boards of directors in your state.) A "board" has legal responsibilities and liabilities, and will probably be required to meet at least once a year and record minutes of their meetings.

Members of the board of directors have a fiduciary duty to protect the interests of the shareholders of the company — not to protect you. They can control the decisions about management of the company even if you own a controlling interest in the stock.

Who should you ask to be on your board? The board of directors makes legally-binding decisions for the company, so be very careful about who you choose for board members. If you have investors, especially venture capitalists, they'll expect to be on the board, and you will probably have no choice but to include them.

If you are able to secure well-known individuals from your industry, or a related industry, it adds stature to your company and helps you be perceived as a leader.

The best board members are those who understand your business, are supportive of you (even when they challenge particular decisions), have a long-range view of your company's growth, and bring excellent connections to the business or financial world.

Advisory Committee: This is an informal group with no legal authority, no liability, and no set rules about when to meet or how many people must be involved. In fact, they don't ever have to meet; your advisory committee can simply be a few people who've agreed to let you turn to them for advice.

The point of having advisors is to seek advice, so look for people whose advice you trust to serve on your committee. Ideally you'll find wise folks who are also seasoned entrepreneurs from your industry. Be wary of asking potential investors, customers, employees, or, naturally, competitors. You don't need many advisors, and you don't have to ask everybody at once.

Most people willing to be an advisor aren't motivated by money — they're motivated to help you succeed. Granting stock is the usual form of compensation; that way, they share in your success. And, of course, make sure your advisors get any company trinkets — t-shirts, coffee mugs, pens, etc.

MY SUPPORT SYSTEM

Use this worksheet to list the names or sources of people or organizations you can turn to for support and advice. You may list people who have already committed to supporting you, or list potential supporters you want to ask for help in the future.

Business Buddies:

Mentors:

Entrepreneurs' Groups:

Industry Groups:

Advisory Committee Members:

Board Members:

Others:

MY TEAM: HOW DO I MANAGE EMPLOYEES?

When you run a small company, you can't afford to waste resources, yet many business owners often squander one of their most valuable assets: their employees. I'm always surprised when I encounter an employer who views having employees as a necessary evil to be endured rather than a resource to be developed. If you waste the intelligence, energy, or skills of employees, it's just like throwing money out the window.

But having employees is also a challenge. You have to deal with state and federal labor laws, paperwork, and all those personalities! Some of your time is going to be diverted from specific tasks to personality issues — how people get along, communicate, and solve problems. It takes time. In a small company, it often seems easier just to do things yourself rather than take the time to find, hire, train, and manage employees.

Your attitude towards the people you hire goes a long way in determining their attitude about the job they do. The surest way to get the most from employees is to treat each with respect. No matter what kind of work a person does, they like to have a sense that their opinion and input counts. When you allow your employees to think about how to solve problems, not just carry out specific tasks, you can unleash an amazing amount of creativity and energy.

Employee Policies

Once you hire your first employee, you'll need a set of personnel policies. Even in a very small company, a written set of policies helps create a sense of security and fairness for employees. But developing company policies doesn't mean you need a five-inch thick rule book.

As you develop your company policies, be clear, allow flexibility when you can, and above all, be fair. Treating people fairly does not necessarily mean treating people equally: a salesperson may need a paid cell phone; a stockroom clerk may not. An

employee with a terminally-ill relative may need more flexible work schedules than others. Part of your job as an employer is to constantly examine your own actions for bias. Apply the same standards — not the same rules — to all.

Sometimes you can't be flexible — rules have to be followed. This is particularly true when company policy is dictated by law. When you have to follow inflexible rules, let employees know why. Is it for safety, to obey laws, or to meet certain standards? Help people understand why a rule isn't silly.

Use the worksheet on pages 84–85 to establish the main policies your business will follow in dealing with employees.

For more information on federal and state laws that affect treatment of personnel, consult Michael Jenkins' *Starting and Operating a Business in the U.S.,* published by Running 'R' Media, or www.RhondaWorks.com.

Compensation and Incentives

To attract good employees, you have to offer a salary and benefits that are at least competitive with similar businesses in your area. Most employees are attracted first by the salary or wage offered, but they will also decide to accept a job based on the total "package," including:

- Base salary/wage
- Bonuses, based either on individual performance, group or company performance, or guaranteed bonus;
- Overtime, which may be set by law;
- Signing bonus, as an incentive to an applicant in a very tight job market;
- Commissions, given on sales made;
- Profit sharing, a portion of the overall company profits;

> ### Rhonda's Rule
> **hire people you trust and trust them**

RED TAPE ALERT!

Federal and state governments impose several laws on compensation, treatment, and protection of employees. Among the many regulations your business must follow are the following:

- Tax withholdings, including income, social security, and unemployment taxes
- Insurance requirements, including workers' compensation insurance and "COBRA" requirements
- OSHA safety rules and recordkeeping
- ERISA employee benefit rules
- Anti-discrimination laws
- Immigration laws
- Minimum wage and hour laws and child labor laws
- Family and medical leave laws
- Employee vs. independent contractor distinctions

■ Stock options or stock purchase plans, giving the employee a discounted means to purchase a direct financial stake in the company.

To determine the "going rate" for compensation packages in your industry and region, consult human resource/personnel specialists and other businesspeople. In tight labor markets, you're obviously going to have to offer higher salaries and benefits.

Benefits: In addition to direct cash payments and/or stock, most jobs offer a range of other benefits. Typically, these include paid vacation, health insurance, and retirement benefits. Large companies may offer a wider range of benefits than smaller or newer companies, but this isn't always the case, and good employees expect at least a decent package of basic benefits.

Benefits can be powerful motivators for employees. But devising a benefits package is not necessarily easy. Besides the cost of benefits (especially such things as health insurance) there are questions of fairness, such as whether employees' children should be covered. If so, should childless employees receive an equal total dollar benefit package?

Sometimes small perks are appreciated, such as free drinks, snacks, or other food. "Creative" perks often appeal to certain employees. The most motivating benefit may be flexibility. An applicant may want to start work at 10 AM to avoid rush hour or leave work at 3:30 PM to be home with the kids after school.

The "Personnel Policies" worksheet on pages 84–85 includes space to list insurance and other benefits you want to offer employees.

Training: Just as you have to continually improve your own skills and abilities, you want to continually improve the capabilities of your employees. The best companies make a strong commitment to ongoing training and education.

Often the easiest way to provide training, especially for a small company, is to pay for employees to attend outside seminars or classes. These are offered by a wide range of providers. As your company grows, you may want to develop some in-house training programs or bring in seminar leaders or speakers.

Don't just provide training for specific skills. While these may be necessary, it's also beneficial to educate employees in other, broader areas, such as overall

MY PERSONNEL POLICIES

Always check with an attorney or human resources specialist before finalizing your personnel policies, as state and federal laws may affect what you may or may not do regarding overtime, work hours, family leave, etc.

Work Hours

Starting time: _____

Ending time: _____

Flex time policies: _____

Overtime policies: _____

Other: _____

Vacation Days

Number of days per year: _____

When do they become available? _____

Increases after years of service? How many? _____

Can unused vacation days be accumulated? How many? How long?_____
_____

What times of year can they be taken? How do they have to notify you? _____
_____

Sick Leave

How many paid sick days off per year? _____

Can they be accumulated? _____

Special circumstances? _____

Personal Leave

Will you allow any paid personal leave time? How much?   _____
_____

How much notice do employees have to give for personal leave? _____

Holidays

Which holidays will be time off with pay?_____
_____

Any "floating" holidays? _____

Any other time-off policies,either paid or unpaid, sabbaticals, etc.?_____
_____

Reimbursement Policies?

Which expenses will the company reimburse employees for? (e.g., travel, commute, parking, public transportation): _____
_____

How will those have to be documented/submitted? _____
_____

MY PERSONNEL POLICIES

Insurance

List the insurance coverage you'll offer and how and whether dependents are covered:

Health Insurance: _____

Dental Insurance: _____

Vision Insurance: _____

Life Insurance: _____

Disability: _____

Other: _____

Retirement Program

Will you offer a retirement plan? _____

List details: who is covered, when do they vest, what amount employees have to contribute, etc.: _____

_____

_____

Training/Education

What ongoing training will you offer employees?_____

Will you reimburse/pay for non-company-sponsored education/training programs/tuition?

_____

Other: _____

Benefits

List any other special perks/benefits offered (e.g., cell phones, auto leased, birthdays off, etc.):

_____

_____

_____

Employees who are Telecommuting/Home Offices

What reimbursements do you offer them? (e.g., phone, Internet connection, cell phone, office supplies, electricity, furniture allowance, etc.): _____

How do they get reimbursements (submit monthly form or give ongoing amount?):

_____

How many days/weeks are they expected to be at the main office?_____

Other: _____

Performance Review

How often will you do performance reviews? _____

On what basis will performance be judged? _____

Who will participate in reviewing employees? _____

business strategy, industry trends, etc. The smarter, more knowledgeable an employee, the more he or she can contribute to your success.

Rewarding and Acknowledging: Everyone wants acknowledgement for a job well done. Few things are more dispiriting than to excel at a task and have your hard work ignored. It's human nature to be motivated to work harder at pleasing those who appreciate us than those who ignore us. So make it a regular practice to acknowledge and thank every employee who does their job well.

Give credit to all employees who do their job well, with particular rewards for those who perform exceptionally. Give praise quickly and publicly. If you need to discipline an employee, do that privately. Find fun or creative ways to congratulate people. But often, just a public "thank you" or a round of

applause shows that you've noticed their contribution. Take time to celebrate successes, especially with everyone in the company. It's a morale booster.

WHAT KIND OF BOSS WILL I BE?

Being a boss is tough. It's one of the most demanding challenges of running a company. You have to inspire, lead, motivate, discipline, and reward. Some of the most important leadership skills to have are the ability to:

- **Communicate goals:** Let people know why they are doing something, not just how to do it; employees are far more motivated when they understand the purpose of a task;

MY LEADERSHIP SKILLS

Rate yourself in each area below as either: excellent, good, fair, or needs to improve.

SKILL	EXCELLENT	GOOD	FAIR	NEEDS TO IMPROVE
Decision making				
Communicating goals				
Setting standards				
Listening				
Consistently being fair				
Patience				
Creating a learning atmosphere				
Training others				
Motivating others to do their best				
Constructively communicating problems/disagreements				
Acknowledging and rewarding the contributions of others				
Other leadership skills:				

Rhonda's Rule
lead, don't manage

- **Set standards:** You are responsible for establishing — and demonstrating — the standards you expect others to maintain;

- **Be fair:** Make sure your standards are reasonable and fair, and that goals are actually reachable;

- **Listen:** Learn to talk WITH and not just talk TO your employees; enlist their suggestions and set goals together;

- **Make decisions:** The buck has to stop somewhere; employees look to their leaders to make choices and stick with them.

So what kind of boss will you be? Will you have the skills to lead your company rather than micromanage your employees? Can you create an environment that encourages employees to do their best? The Leadership Skills Assessment worksheet on page 86 lets you evaluate your own experiences and abilities as a leader.

WHO DO I NEED ON MY TEAM?

Who are the people most important to your company's future? Who will handle your financial affairs, make sales, plan operations? What roles do you need to fill "in-house" and what jobs can you fill with outside contractors or suppliers?

As you evaluate how your business will grow, look at what managerial roles need to be filled and what kinds of people you'd most like to have fill them. You can then create job descriptions and, assuming you have financing in place, begin recruiting. Use the worksheet on pages 88–89 to identify the positions you need to fill and the specifics of each job.

Independent Contractors

Most companies, especially smaller ones, use outside providers to perform certain tasks. It's not necessary to handle every function — even relatively critical functions — within your own company. You can expand your abilities substantially by turning to others to augment your own staff.

RED TAPE ALERT!

Filling staffing needs with independent contractors rather than employees has advantages, including saving on payroll taxes and administrative headaches. However, be sure that the contractor you hire and the relationship you create meets the federal government's definition of an independent contractor.

The IRS uses a 20-factor test to evaluate whether a person is or is not an employee. The full list is available at their website, www.irs.gov. However, if the contractor you have hired can be described by the following characteristics, beware that he or she may not be considered an independent contractor by the IRS:

- The person works mostly or only for your firm.

- The person is subject to your control, and you direct how and when the work is done, not just the particular result.

- The person works in your office or establishment and does not have his or her own place of business, business cards, or business name.

- The kind of work the person does for you is normally done by employees, such as secretarial work.

- The person is not a licensed professional of any type.

WHO DO I NEED ON MY TEAM?

List the job titles needed in each area. Some suggestions for managers and officers are in parentheses, but you should hire only those your company really needs as it grows.

KEY PERSONNEL	RESPONSIBILITIES	DESIRED EXPERIENCE/ BACKGROUND
Top Management (President/CEO)		
Administrative (Chief Operating Officer)		
Financial (Chief Financial Officer, Controller, bookkeeper, etc.)		
Marketing/Sales/PR (VP Marketing, Director of Sales, PR Director)		
Operations/Production (Production Manager, Inventory Control Mgr)		
Technology (Website developer, Chief Technology Officer, tech support staff)		
Human Resources (Personnel Director)		
Support Staff (e.g. Administrative Assistants, Office Manager)		
Other		

WHO DO I NEED ON MY TEAM?

DESIRED ATTITUDES/ WORK HABITS	DESIRED EDUCATIONAL BACKGROUND	NECESSARY SKILLS	COMPENSATION PACKAGE

ADVERTISING AND LOOKING FOR EMPLOYEES

What recruitment efforts will you use to find employees?

What ongoing training will you offer employees?

What features of your company and/or specific job do you want to mention in your ads?

What unusual or particularly appealing aspects of your company and/or specific job can you describe that would make you stand out from others?

Other aspects to mention in ads or interviews:

List specific places you could advertise/look for employees:

Newspapers: _____

Online career/hiring sites: _____

Schools/Colleges/Universities: _____

Career fairs: _____

Trade organizations: _____

Other organizations: _____

Bulletin boards: _____

Unemployment offices: _____

Other media: _____

Former employees: _____

Other referral sources: _____

Competitors: _____

Others: _____

Outside sources can come in the form of individuals — independent contractors — or other companies. Typically, some of the functions most likely to be outsourced are website hosting, bookkeeping, and graphic design. But you can outsource all kinds of responsibilities: personnel management and recruiting, operations and production, training, and others.

Finding and Hiring Good People

Just as it's easier to be a good parent if you have good kids, it's much easier to be a good boss if you have good employees. When you have an immediate need for an employee, you might be tempted to hire anyone you can get, but it's often better to leave a position unfilled until you can find a person you consider capable and trustworthy.

Hire for attitude, train for skills. In most cases, you can teach a smart and willing person a particular skill (such as a computer program). It's much more difficult to instill the right attitude in the wrong person. And check references! Even if you have no reason to doubt the honesty of an applicant, you can learn a lot by checking references.

It's often very difficult to find enough qualified applicants for a job, especially in a tight labor market. Extend your job-hunting efforts beyond the usual means of a newspaper classified ad. Use the worksheet on page 90 to identify places to seek potential employees.

Summary

Pay attention to choosing, training, developing, and rewarding the people of your company because they are your most important resource. One of the best ways to motivate employees is to make your company an organization they're proud to work for. Employees want to have a sense of purpose and pride in what they do, and they want to work in an environment that respects them and their fellow employees.

QUESTIONS TO ASK . . . POTENTIAL EMPLOYEES

Don't wait until a job applicant is sitting in the waiting room before figuring out what to ask. Take time well before the first interview and make a list of things you'd like to know about someone before you hire them, such as whether they have the right experience, skills, education, etc. Ask specific questions in those areas, "What were your exact responsibilities," "What computer programs did you use regularly," etc. Find out, also, what they liked and didn't like about their previous jobs and what they hope for in their new position. That gives you a better sense of whether they are a good fit for your job and your company.

During interviews, don't do all the talking! It's appropriate to explain the job, and in many cases, to try and 'sell' the job to the candidate, but most of the time the candidate should be talking, not you. You may want to have others also interview the applicant, especially the prospect's direct manager, and possibly co-workers and even people who will work for him or her.

In addition to direct work related questions, it's important to ask questions that give you a sense of the applicant as a person and their attitudes toward responsibility, working as a team, flexibility, etc. But be careful! Some questions are illegal to ask. You can't, for instance, ask whether a candidate is planning on having a child, their marital status, religion, age (in many cases), etc. But it's perfectly legal to ask about hobbies, interests, and long-term goals.

And never, never discriminate on the basis of race, gender, age, national origin, etc. It's not only illegal — you'll eliminate some terrific potential employees.

MY WILD IDEAS

Wild Ideas for Myself:

Wild Ideas for My Advisors:

Wild Ideas for My Team:

money

We each bring our own personal issues to the topic of money. Almost all of us are uncomfortable talking about money. Money, after all, is one of the few things left in modern life we don't discuss openly with even our closest friends or family members.

In a business context, this discomfort with money often extends to a reluctance to deal with budgets, bookkeeping, and accounting. Most of us are intimidated by numbers. (Who, after all, really liked math class?) More often, we just find it unpleasant to have to think about cash flow and profit margins and, especially, debt.

Well, it's time to get over it. Money and numbers are absolutely essential components of business. If you're going to be in business, you must learn to deal with money and numbers in a matter-of-fact, 'business-like' fashion. You have to look at your financial reports without feeling they're a report card of your character, discuss a raise with an employee without feeling you're under attack, and tell a client the price of your services without flinching.

That doesn't mean you should start boasting about every dollar you make or obsess about every line of your budget. It's more about developing a healthy understanding and respect for the part that money and numbers play in your business.

UNDERSTANDING THE NUMBERS

People in business usually fall into one of two categories — those who are fascinated with numbers, and those who are frightened by them. If you're in the second category, you're probably intimidated by the very prospect of having to fill in the forms in this section.

Take heart. Numbers are neither magical, mysterious, nor menacing. They merely reflect decisions you have already made in your business planning process. Every decision leads to a number, but numbers themselves are not decisions. You cannot pull a number out of thin air because the financial forms call for a specific figure on a specific line.

Begin your financial planning with these simple steps:

- **Prepare a budget and other financial documents.** If yours is a small business, you may only need to prepare a simple budget: a forecast of your estimated sales and a list of how much you

> ## Rhonda's Rule
> **numbers are simply reflections of decisions you have already made**

plan to spend on the various components of your business. For a larger company, or if you're seeking outside financing, you'll need a range of financial documents to help you determine or adjust your spending and marketing habits.

- **Consult an accountant.** Even before you start your business, sit down and meet with an accountant. Some expenses must be considered "start-up costs" and have different tax treatment than expenses you incur once you're actually operating a business. An accountant will help you with these details. Use the guide "Questions to Ask... An Accountant" below when you meet with your accountant the first time.

- **Set up books.** Get a good bookkeeping/accounting software program or bookkeeping service. Ask your accountant to give you advice.

The worksheets in this section of your Organizer will help you with these steps. Begin with learning the language of money.

Know the Lingo

To make talking about money a bit easier, use this list of money-related buzzwords. Soon you'll sound like you've been discussing money for decades:

- **"Red ink" or "in the red."** On accounting ledgers, negative numbers used to be written in red ink. So the expressions "red ink" or "in the red" refer to showing a loss.

- **"In the black."** Positive numbers, on the other hand, were written in black ink. So if your accounts finish "in the black," you've come out with a profit.

- **Your "nut."** This term refers to your monthly overhead or fixed expenses, the amount of money you're obligated to spend each month regardless of sales. This includes rent, salaries, utilities, and insurance.

- **Your "burn rate."** This is how much money you're going through. This can be different than your fixed expenses, depending on what you spend on variable expenses, such as marketing, temporary help, buying new equipment, etc.

- **The "bottom line."** At the top of your financial statements, you list your income. You then deduct your expenses. The number you're left with on the last line of your profit and loss statement is how much money you've made — or lost. That's your company's "bottom line."

The following section and worksheets will help you budget from the "bottom up."

QUESTIONS TO ASK... AN ACCOUNTANT

- What kinds of taxes will I have to pay? What are my tax deadlines?
- How can I reduce my taxes? Which expenses are deductible, non-deductible or have to be depreciated?
- What kind of bookkeeping system should I set up? How can I set up systems to reduce the possibility of theft or embezzlement?
- What kind of retirement program can I set up and how much can I contribute each year? What kind of retirement programs for my employees?
- What are the advantages and disadvantages of different kinds of corporate forms for my type of business?
- How should I pay myself — salary or draw — and what are the tax implications?
- Should I use the cash or accrual form of bookkeeping?
- What other accounting and tax considerations are there for my type business?

WHERE DO I GET MY NUMBERS?

The key to financial planning is to create your financial projections after or at the same time you plan your business. If you choose to locate your business in one town versus another, there's a cost associated with that. If you exhibit at a trade show, there's a cost with that. Again, your numbers, your projections of your income and expenses, are reflections of decisions you make.

Budgeting Strategies

Successful financial projections are achieved by budgeting from the "bottom up," not the "top down."

"Top down" numbers are enticing to work with because they always come out looking good, but they're not realistic. Here's how they work: you look at the big picture — the total market size, growth rate, average sales price, and average profit margins. You make what seem to be reasonable assumptions, something like achieving a 10% market penetration, or improving margins by 2%. Then you fill in each line of your financial statements to make the totals come out to the big numbers projected.

For example, let's say you've invented a new, improved golf club, and you project you will achieve at least 1% market penetration within 3 years. If total annual sales of golf clubs is $2 billion, then you plan to achieve $20 million in annual sales. With a profit margin of 15%, you will have a net profit of $3 million.

Sounds good, doesn't it? "Top down" projections result in some very positive numbers — the kind that make you and perhaps some potential investors excited. They're just not very realistic. And they're indefensible when investors start asking tough questions.

Instead, the best financials are developed from the "bottom up." You do the real business-building legwork: examine different distribution channels, source manufacturers and suppliers, develop a staffing chart, outline your marketing program, and design operations. You plug in numbers from these realistic projections of how much things will cost,

and then determine how much income you need to sustain that cost.

So, let's say you're that same golf club manufacturer, and you're building your financials from the "bottom up," here's how it would work:

You first compare different distribution channels, and then choose one. Let's say you decide to sell through specialty golf retailers and country clubs. This channel has associated costs and impact on income. You'll need to budget for a sales force to sell to those shops, exhibit at the annual sporting good trade shows, and advertise in *Golf Retailer* magazine. But you will only receive 40–45% of the final sales price of the club, since the retailer takes half and the salesperson receives a commission.

Now, you're starting to get real numbers to plug in to each of the lines of your financial forms. You've got numbers for advertising, staffing, and income.

Researching the Numbers

All this planning takes work, but there's help. The best place to start is by speaking with others in your industry, attending trade shows, and contacting your industry association.

Another good method for making financial forecasts is to use the worksheets in this book. Beginning on page 96 are 4 worksheets that will help you develop a comprehensive set of financial statements: Sales Projections, Marketing Budget, Profit & Loss Statement, and Cash Flow Projection. You can then use these in your business plan as well.

Another good source of help in preparing financial forms, especially ones you'll need to show investors, is the Abrams Method of Flow Through Financials in my book *The Successful Business Plan: Secrets & Strategies.* Or consult my website, www.RhondaWorks.com, for helpful links and budgeting tools.

Rhonda's Rule

always underestimate income and overestimate expenses

SALES PROJECTIONS

	Monthly First Year	Total First Year	Monthly Second Year	Total Second Year	Monthly Third Year	Total Third Year
Product Line #1						
Unit Volume						
Unit Price						
Commissions						
Returns and Allowances						
Gross Revenue						
Net Revenue						
Product Line #2						
Unit Volume						
Unit Price						
Commissions						
Returns and Allowances						
Gross Revenue						
Net Revenue						
Product Line #3						
Unit Volume						
Unit Price						
Commissions						
Returns and Allowances						
Gross Revenue						
Net Revenue						
Product Line #4						
Unit Volume						
Unit Price						
Commissions						
Returns and Allowances						
Gross Revenue						
Net Revenue						
TOTALS FOR ALL PRODUCT LINES						
Unit Volume						
Unit Price						
Commissions						
Returns and Allowances						
Gross Revenue						
TOTAL NET REVENUE (enter on page 98)						

MARKETING BUDGET

	Monthly First Year	Total First Year	Monthly Second Year	Total Second Year	Monthly Third Year	Total Third Year
Professional Assistance						
Marketing/PR Consultants						
Advertising Agencies						
Direct Mail Specialists						
Graphic Design						
Brochures/Leaflets/Flyers						
Merchandising Displays						
Sampling/Premiums						
Media Advertising						
Print						
Online						
Television and Radio						
Other Media						
Phone Directories						
Advertising Specialties						
Direct Mail						
Printing						
List Purchases						
Postage						
Mailing House						
Website						
Maintenance & Hosting						
Trade Shows						
Fees and Setup						
Travel/Shipping						
Exhibits/Signs						
PR Activities						
Informal Marketing/ Networking						
Memberships						
Entertainment						
Other:						
TOTAL (enter on page 98)						

PROFIT & LOSS STATEMENT: ANNUAL BY MONTH

For Year: _____	January	February	March	April	May
INCOME					
Gross Sales					
Less returns and allowances					
Net Sales (from page 96)					
Cost of Goods					
GROSS PROFIT					
General and Administrative Expenses					
Salaries and wages					
Employee benefits					
Payroll Taxes					
Sales commissions					
Professional services					
Rent					
Maintenance					
Equipment Rental					
Furniture and Equipment purchase					
Depreciation and amortization					
Insurance					
Interest expenses					
Utilities					
Telephone / Telecommunications					
Office supplies					
Postage and shipping					
Marketing/Advertising (from page 97)					
Travel					
Entertainment					
Other:					
Other:					
Other:					
TOTAL G & A EXPENSES					
Net Income before Taxes					
Provision for taxes on income					
NET INCOME AFTER TAXES (NET PROFIT)					

PROFIT & LOSS STATEMENT – CONTINUED

June	July	August	September	October	November	December	TOTAL

CASH FLOW PROJECTION

For Year: _____	January	February	March	April	May
CASH RECEIPTS					
Income from Sales					
Cash Sales					
Collections					
Total Cash from Sales					
Income from Financing					
Interest Income					
Loan Proceeds					
Total Cash from Financing					
Other Cash Receipts					
TOTAL CASH RECEIPTS					

CASH DISBURSEMENTS					
Expenses					
Cost of Goods					
Operating Expenses					
Loan Payments					
Income Tax Payments					
Other Expenses/Equip Purchase					
Reserve					
Owner's Draw					
TOTAL CASH DISBURSEMENTS					

NET CASH FLOW					
Opening Cash Balance					
Total Cash Receipts					
less Total Cash Disbursements					
ENDING CASH BALANCE					

CASH FLOW PROJECTION – CONTINUED

June	July	August	September	October	November	December	TOTAL

WHAT WOULD RHONDA DO . . . TO SET UP ACCOUNTS

Having tried a few different accounting programs, I'd use QuickBooks if my computer was a PC, and MYOB if I have a Mac (because QuickBooks had not updated its Mac version at the time of this writing). I'd purchase the QuickBooks Premiere Tech Support and use it. I'd have a reliable employee enter and manage the accounts instead of a more costly bookkeeper, but still use my accountant do my tax planning and preparation, set up my account categories, and regularly review my accounts. I'd explore online accounting services. And I'd take all those receipts out of my shoe-box.

Setting up Accounts/"Books"

My first set of company "books" was a simple lined ledger book. On one set of pages, I wrote down all my total income as I received it; on other pages I wrote down each time I billed a client and their payments; and on another set of pages I wrote down my expenses (at least as frequently as I remembered to sit down and enter them). This was hardly the most efficient way to keep accounts, but at least I could see how much money I had made, how much each client owed me, and, at the end of the year, how much to deduct when preparing taxes.

Things have improved since then. Simple and inexpensive computer programs enable you to keep track of your expenses, income, and billing, prepare financial reports instantly, and prepare your taxes. Many of these services are available on the Internet, so you can access them wherever you are.

If yours is a very small business, you may be able to handle all your bookkeeping needs with a personal check-book/money-management program like Quicken. But many businesses need a more robust accounting program, like QuickBooks, MYOB, or Peachtree.

One of the first things you'll need to do is determine whether you will keep your accounts on a "cash" or on an "accrual" basis.

- **Cash basis:** When you operate your business on a cash basis, you enter expenses and income as they actually are paid or received. This is the easiest kind of accounting, and most smaller companies can be handled on a cash basis.

- **Accrual basis:** With an accrual accounting system, you enter expenses and income as they are incurred.

If you sign a contract for a purchase in January but don't pay until March, that expense would show up on your books in January on an accrual basis but in March on a cash basis, and this has tax and profit implications. Many companies are not permitted to operate on a cash basis, especially those with inventories of goods. Once again, talk to you accountant.

Establishing a Bank Account

A good relationship with a bank can be a big help to a growing company. Many people just select the bank located close to them, or the one with the lowest fees on accounts. Ideally, you want a bank that will work with you and your company as you grow, that will provide some understanding of your situation and allow some flexibility in dealing with you.

Take some time to "shop" for a bank for your business. The worksheet on page 103 can help you compare banks and banking services.

Cash Flow

If the three most important things in real estate are "location, location, location," the first three rules of business are "cash, cash, cash." It's necessary, of course,

---

Rhonda's Rule
cash counts, so always count your cash

BANK COMPARISON CHART

	BANK	BANK	BANK
Bank name			
Location/Phone number			
Name of bank rep. handling business accounts			
Accounts offered and fees charged			
Loan or credit lines available			
Special business services offered			
Your overall impression of this bank and its services			
Other notes:			

RHONDA'S MONEY MANAGEMENT TIPS

- **Review your books regularly.** When you're running your business, you may not take the time to sit down and look at your financials. But you can't manage your money without having the facts. At least once a month, preferably once a week, look at your figures: accounts payable and receivable, expenses, cash flow, etc.

- **Send them your bill!** I'm always surprised by how many businesspeople, especially consultants and professional service providers, delay sending out their invoices. You may feel uncomfortable asking someone for money, afraid of being challenged on how much you've billed, or just too busy working than billing for it. But the longer you wait to send out your invoices, the greater the chance you won't get paid.

- **Watch your inventory.** If you produce goods, you'll always be tempted to produce more because you get savings based on volume. But inventory can go "bad" — become outdated, unsaleable, time- or weather-worn. Inventory doesn't just apply to finished goods for resale. You may have "inventory" in the form of marketing materials. Keep an eye on your actual use and make your purchases not only on the basis of price but whether you can get small quantities only when you actually need them.

- **Manage your growth.** You want your business to get bigger, but if you grow too fast you may not be able to sustain it. Growth costs money, as you incur many expenses before you see additional income. As much as possible, plan your growth, so you have the financial resources to pay for it.

- **Save.** Every business has income fluctuations. The best way to have cash when you need it is to put some away when you've got it.

to be profitable, but "profit" is a number that shows up on your accounts at the end of the year; cash is money you have in the bank. In a small company, it's cash that determines whether you can pay your bills.

No matter what your business is, you're going to have a lag between outgo and income. If you're a consultant, you have to pay for your phone, stationery, marketing materials, and rent before you get your first client. Once you've got them, you're not going to see complete payment for at least 30–60 days after you finish a project. Things are much worse if you're a manufacturer. You've got to pay for raw material, equipment, and employees many months before you'll see final payment.

Rhonda's Rule
you can't get money in unless you get your invoices out

So draw up a cash flow projection. Even if you don't write up a budget or income statement, it's a good idea to sketch out when you expect money to come in and when you need money to go out.

Use the "Cash Flow Projection" worksheet on pages 100–101 to forecast your cash needs.

HOW MUCH SHOULD I CHARGE?

An old joke: A store owner purchases pencils for ten cents a piece and then sells them for a nickel. Noticing this bizarre behavior, his partner asks, "How do you expect us to stay in business that way?" The man replies, "Volume!"

Surprisingly, many novice entrepreneurs choose a relatively similar business strategy. They imagine all that's necessary for success is to price their products or services cheaper than the competition. Low prices, they assume, will generate sufficient sales to more than make up for smaller profits.

Competing on price is risky business. Some discount outlets do build thriving businesses on low prices, but this strategy almost always means narrow profit margins, which in turn means less cash floating around your company. With a small financial cushion, you're vulnerable with every slight increase in costs. The landlord raises your rent 5%? That may be your entire year's profit. And you're at risk from competitors: if you become a serious threat and they have deeper cash reserves, they can just undercut your prices and wait until you're squeezed out of the market.

Moreover, customers attracted solely by price are fickle. If they shopped around a lot before choosing you, they're probably going to continually be shopping around.

Setting Professional Service Fees

Another old joke: A machine in a factory breaks, shutting down production, costing the company thousands of dollars an hour. In desperation, the owner calls a consultant to determine the problem. The expert spends five minutes examining the machine, changes one small part, and presto! The machine works. When the owner gets a bill from the consultant for $10,000, he's outraged. "Ten thousand dollars for five minutes and a five dollar part!" So, he asks for an itemized bill. The consultant sends back the following invoice:

Parts	$5.00
Time	$5.00
Knowing which part to fix:	$9,990.00

When what you're selling is your expertise, setting fees is often more an art than a science. The two

---

Rhonda's Rule

the ultimate price is the price customers are willing to pay

---

main ways of pricing services are on an "hourly" basis or on a "project" basis.

- **Hourly:** An hourly fee basis rewards you appropriately when you have long, complicated tasks, but short-changes you when what you're selling is your existing knowledge or expertise.

- **Project:** On a "project" or task basis, you establish a set or minimum fee for an entire project. Clients often like working on a project basis because they like knowing what they will be paying up-front. Project fees reward you when your knowledge enables you to finish projects quickly but penalizes you if you've badly misjudged the amount of time a given project will take.

One way to establish fees is to determine typical fees charged by others for similar services. The comparison chart of competitors' prices on page 107 can help you with this. Based on your experience and your specialty, you should be able to get pretty close to an appropriate fee. Call a professional or trade organization, ideally in your area, to get a sense of typical fee structures.

In the final analysis, the appropriate fee is always the same: what the market will bear.

Setting Prices for Goods and Other Services

If you are a retailer or reseller of products or services produced by others, it's often relatively easy to figure out how much to charge. Most industries have generally accepted mark-ups over the cost of goods (for example, 100% in department stores, 200% for jewelry, etc.).

Of course, many successful companies have been built by not following industry norms, such as wholesale clubs. But understanding normal practice in your industry is a good place to start when figuring how much you want to charge. Suppliers themselves will often let you know what the normal mark-up is on their goods (but be careful — there are some laws limiting suppliers from setting the final prices of their goods).

If you are the manufacturer or producer of goods or services sold by others, the reseller will set the final price to the end-user. If your costs to the reseller are too high, then they won't be able to make money and won't purchase from you. It's critical for you to know what your competitors are charging those same resellers.

Of course, you have to cover your costs and make a profit. And that's typically how manufacturers and others set prices. Once again, this is "bottom-up" planning: figure your costs for raw materials, labor, overhead, shipping, returns, etc., and then set a reasonable figure for profit. But that number should be in line with what resellers are willing to pay and what the competition is charging. If you are far off, you either have a radical new business model or more likely have misjudged the situation.

Brilliant businesspeople have built great companies by knowing how to lower prices or convince customers to pay higher prices. Most of us, however, need to stick to the normal range when planning our businesses.

Use the comparison chart on page 107 to research what your competitors charge. If you can, find out what their costs are, and research on what basis they compete with you other than price.

HOW DO I RAISE MONEY TO START OR GROW?

Ask an entrepreneur starting or expanding a business to name their biggest problem, and you'll probably hear: "Where do I get the money?"

What may come as a shock, especially if you're new to business, is how long it's going to take to raise the money you need or to reach a level of income where your business can pay its own way. Just because you're in a hurry to get money doesn't mean investors or lenders share your sense of urgency.

One basic difference you must know before looking for money is the difference between "debt" and "equity."

- **Debt:** This is usually a loan, line of credit, or equipment financing, and it must be paid back, whether or not the business does well. You often begin making payments on the debt soon after receiving the loan ("debt service") so you have an additional monthly expense. You give up no ownership of the company, however.

- **Equity:** This is usually referred to as getting an "investment." With equity financing, you give an investor a piece of the ownership of the company and a share of future profits and, often, a say in decision-making. If the company fails, however, you do not have to pay anyone back.

There are also a few forms of financing that combine the two, such as "convertible debt" in which a loan can be turned into stock. If you or your investors/lenders want to explore some of these options, consult an attorney or accountant.

Whose Money Do You Want?

Not all money is equal. When you first start to look for financing, you might be tempted to take any money you can find, but you should exercise care. The various sources of money seek different rates of return on their investments, have varying levels of sophistication and comfort with risk, and provide you with significantly different advantages and disadvantages. And you are going to have an ongoing relationship with your money source. You'll save yourself a lot of time and grief if you seek money only from sources that are right for you.

The main funding sources for starting or expanding a business are:

Your Own Assets: Forget the old saying about using "other people's money." It's better to start or grow a business with your own money. If you have sufficient assets, particularly savings or other income that don't require you to take on additional debt, you're in the best financial position. You don't go into debt, and you don't give up equity. If your savings are owned jointly with a spouse or partner, be certain to get their acceptance and understanding of your plans.

COMPETITORS' PRICE COMPARISON CHART

	Product/Service #1	Product/Service #2	Product/Service #3
Competitor A			
Competitor's price:			
Competitor's costs (if known):			
Basis for competitor's advantage (if any):			

Competitor B			
Competitor's price:			
Competitor's costs (if known):			
Basis for competitor's advantage (if any):			

Competitor C			
Competitor's price:			
Competitor's costs (if known):			
Basis for competitor's advantage (if any):			

On page 109 you'll find the worksheet "What Are my Existing Assets?" to help you assess your own financial picture.

Sales/Income. The very best way to fund a business is from sales revenues. If you can grow your company based on money received from customers, then you don't take on debt and you don't give up equity. This is not as impossible as it sounds, especially if you are starting a low-cost business. The key is to try to line up clients before you actually set up shop, and to grow only as big as your revenues permit. Your growth may be slower, and it doesn't seem as sexy as getting a huge investment, but you'll sleep better at night.

Strategic Partners. There are many other businesses that might want you to succeed and be willing to help. Perhaps they are a potential supplier, customer, or business serving the same market. In some cases, they might directly invest in your business or give you loans or other financing. Perhaps they would let you use their offices or equipment or otherwise help offset some of your expenses in return for the benefits you bring them. See the chapter on "My Competitive Edge" for more on finding strategic partners.

Credit Cards. Experts will tell you credit cards are a terrible way to finance a business — high interest, personal risk, etc. They're right — if you have other alternatives. The truth is most people use credit cards at one time or another to pay business expenses, particularly in the start-up phase. And credit cards can be a useful way to handle short-term cash flow problems; if you realistically expect income soon, credit cards may be an easier or better alternative than other loans or taking on an investor.

But be careful! Credit cards are generally an expensive form of financing (exceptions are low introductory rates). You can incur very high charges if you are even a day or two late on your payments. Credit card debt easily gets out of hand, and you have to pay the money back.

Use the worksheet "My Credit Cards" on page 110 to keep track of the credit cards you have and manage payments. You can enter due dates into your "To Do" list at www.RhondaWorks.com to receive an e-mailed reminder.

Friends and Family. Want to lose a friend? Borrow money from them. Getting family or friends involved in your business is dangerous, but there are exceptions. If the person understands your business, truly comprehends the risks, and is someone with whom you can communicate well, the situation may work. Always have loan or investment papers drawn up with the terms of the repayment or investment absolutely clear.

"Angels." Angel is the term applied to private individuals who invest their own money in new compa-

---

QUESTIONS TO ASK . . . BEFORE YOU ACCEPT FINANCING

- Are you willing to give up some amount of ownership of your company?
- Are you willing to have debt that you have to repay?
- Are you willing to risk property or other assets?
- How much control of the direction and operation of your company are you willing to relinquish?
- What other help do you want from a funder besides money?
- How fast do you want to grow?
- How big do you want your company to be?
- What do you see as the long-term relationship between you and your funding source?

TAKING STOCK: WHAT ARE MY EXISTING ASSETS?

	SPECIFICS (amount, type, etc.)	HOW READILY AVAILABLE
Financial Assets:		
Savings		
Income from Other Sources		
Spouses Income		
Credit Lines/Credit Cards		
Stocks & Other liquid assets		
Home equity		
Retirement funds		
Other		
Tangible Assets:		
Equipment		
Furniture		
Space/Location		
Other		
Business/Professional Assets:		
Marketable skills		
Specialized Knowledge		
Business experience		
Certifications/Credentials		
Licenses, Memberships		
Ability to make sales		
Good customers/client relationships		
Other		
Personal Assets:		
Education/Training		
Intelligence		
Excellent Communication Skills		
Outstanding Work Habits		
Business or Financial Connections		
Rich Relatives or friends		
Supportive Family and/or Friends		
Ambition & Passion		
Other		

MY CREDIT CARDS

Every business relies on credit cards — but some more than others. You may be relying on credit cards to help finance some of your start-up costs, such as equipment purchases. You may also need to manage your credit card debt before or after you start your business to make sure you have a clean credit report. Use this space to track credit card offers, credit cards you already have, credit card debt you need to pay off, or other useful information about your credit cards.

Name of Card Issuer	Card Number	Credit Limit	Interest	Other Fees	Current Balance

RED TAPE ALERT!

A no-interest loan from a friend or family member may face what's called "imputed interest" by the IRS. The lender may not be receiving any interest from you, but the IRS will tax them as if they were. If the IRS views the loan as a gift, the lender is subject to federal gift tax rules and will have to pay taxes on the money if it is more than the maximum allowed by law. The lender must charge an interest rate that reflects a fair market value.

nies. Because it is their own money, they often have a wider range of kinds of companies they'll invest in, and seek more diverse types of returns on their investment, than professional investors such as venture capitalists. They usually invest a smaller amount of money than professional sources. Angels are generally much more accessible and more appropriate for small companies. A number of "angel networks" or organizations have sprung up in large cities. Accountants, financial planners, lawyers, or bankers may also be able to help you identify potential angels, or check www.RhondaWorks.com for angel contacts.

Banks. Realistically, banks loan money only to companies that have been in business for at least one or two years and have been successful. As your company grows, you'll almost certainly want a line of credit from a bank to help you manage your cash and payments. If you do get a bank loan for a new business, you'll probably have to put up personal assets as collateral. The Small Business Administration provides loan guarantees to banks to encourage them to make small business loans. To find out more about SBA loans, visit www.sba.gov.

Venture Capitalists. Venture capitalists are professional investors using institutional money. They generally only invest in companies needing substantial sums of money to grow very large very quickly, and that will serve very large markets. They do provide early stage investments as well as financing for companies that are growing. They are particularly active in technology-related businesses. VCs have high expectations of return on their investment but are willing to take substantial risks. VCs take an active role in managing the companies they invest in, often even replacing or removing the founders from management.

The comparison chart on the following pages helps you decide whose money you want. Consider your various financing sources, and answer the questions to find the one that suits you and your business best.

Creating a Business Plan

If you're going to seek funds from outside investors — and in many cases even from lenders — you'll need a business plan. A business plan is a document that outlines your entire business strategy, financing, competition, staffing, future developments, and the steps necessary to achieve your results. It's different from an operating plan, which is designed primarily to help company management organize day-to-day activities.

An outline of a business plan is included on pages 233–235. In addition, the companion guide to this Organizer, *The Successful Business Plan: Secrets & Strategies,* leads you step-by-step through the process of writing a business plan and looking for funding.

PAYING TAXES!

Nobody likes paying taxes, but you're going to have to pay them. In fact, the more successful you are, the more taxes you'll probably pay.

Understanding key tax concerns is critical for most businesses. You will make some decisions — or alter them — based on tax implications.

Some business expenses are fully deductible, others are only partially deductible, others have to be depreciated over a number of years, and others are

INVESTOR COMPARISON CHART

QUESTIONS	INVESTOR	INVESTOR
Investor's Name		
Contact Info (e-mail, phone, address, fax)		
What type of investor is this? (venture capitalist, angel, friend or family, other)		
What industries do they invest in?		
What stage of companies do they invest in? (seed, startup, second round, etc.)		
What range of amount of investment do they make?		
What geographic areas do they invest in?		
What are their other criteria for investment?		
What other companies have they invested in?		
Who do I know who can help me reach this investor?		
How do they prefer to be contacted?		
Other:		

INVESTOR COMPARISON CHART

INVESTOR	INVESTOR	INVESTOR

MY TAX DEADLINES

You may face a variety of different tax obligations. If you enter these in your "To Do" list at www.RhondaWorks.com, Rhonda will send you an e-mail reminder.

Tax	Amount	Where to Send/File	Dates Due
Income tax: federal, state, county, perhaps local (e.g. New York City)			
Payroll and other employment-related taxes (Social Security, worker's compensation, unemployment, etc.)			
Sales tax			
Personal property tax and use taxes			
Property tax			
Special taxes (hotel, food, transportation, etc.)			
Business taxes			
Import/export, custom taxes and duties			
Transfer taxes			
Capital gains taxes			
Inventory taxes			
Other:			

not deductible at all. You should have at least a fair understanding of those issues as you make choices in your business. If you purchase a very expensive piece of equipment, for instance, expecting to deduct the total cost of that from your income, you may be rudely surprised that the expense has to be spread out over as many as ten to twenty years. Also, your tax obligation may change depending on when and how you receive certain types of income.

Tax codes are complicated and always changing. Certain tax laws apply to incorporated businesses and not unincorporated ones, or vice versa, and business tax laws differ from regulations for individuals. And of course, every U.S. state has its own tax laws as well.

You need an accountant to help you plan, manage, and understand your taxes. Ideally, tax planning should begin even before you start business, especially as some early decisions may have a major impact on your status — what legal form you establish for your company, such as corporation versus partnership, whether you operate on a cash or an accrual basis, etc.

Many businesspeople find it helpful to set up separate savings accounts just for taxes. With each check they receive, they set aside a certain percentage in this separate tax account, so when tax time comes they have the money necessary.

As a business, you often have responsibility for collecting and then paying taxes owed by others. For instance, if you are a retailer, you must charge and collect the sales tax on items you sell to consumers. Set up records to keep track of those taxes that you've collected — and pay them by the dates due. You may want to — or sometimes be required to — set up separate accounts to keep the taxes you collect distinct from your other funds. Governments, whether federal, state, or city, really frown on you keeping their money.

You may be surprised by the variety of taxes you face. There are income taxes, sales taxes, payroll taxes, property taxes, personal property taxes, inventory taxes, special use taxes, general business taxes,

and others. Some taxes incur substantial penalties for late or under payments, so be certain to keep track of when taxes are due and give yourself enough time to prepare them.

The worksheet on page 114 can help you keep track of your tax obligations and due dates.

HOW SHOULD I PREPARE FOR THE FUTURE?

A final note about money. When you're just starting a business, or in the midst of expanding a company, you're unlikely to be thinking a lot about your retirement. But you need to consider retirement programs for both you and your employees.

Retirement Plans

There are many types of retirement plans available for both self-employed individuals and businesses. Some of these receive extremely favorable tax treatment, allowing you or your employees to "shelter" some current income (not pay tax on it now) and delay taxes until after retirement. Others allow you to pay tax on income now but shelter all the financial gain on the dollars you set aside for retirement.

Even if you are relatively new to business and your income isn't very high yet, you should look into retirement plans. If you are a one-person business, you may find substantial tax savings by establishing a self-employment retirement plan.

Summary

Money is at the heart of every business, and understanding money — how to raise it, account for it, and manage it — is critical to business success. You will need the assistance of a good, qualified accountant to help you in most aspects of managing your money, particularly tax planning and preparation and setting up your accounting procedures and books. Stay on top of your finances. Set up controls to protect you against theft. And learn that numbers aren't mystical symbols, but important signposts helping you understand your business decisions.

MY WILD IDEAS

Wild Ideas for Making Money:

Wild Ideas for Raising Money:

Wild Ideas for Managing Money:

operations
& administration

How are you going to make this business happen? Whether you are starting or growing a company, sooner or later your new or bigger business will need a home, equipment, and an efficient way to produce and distribute the things you make or the services you provide.

Where will you work, make, or sell your products? What kind of equipment do you need? How will you keep track of paperwork? Even something as basic as a desk and a chair can turn your business into a reality, but which desk? Which chair?

Few entrepreneurs like to deal with the mundane details of running a company. You probably started your business because you enjoyed providing your product or service — not because you liked hanging lights over your desk, picking out a conference table, or negotiating contracts with suppliers and distributors. As your business grows, or you add a new product line or change a distribution channel, the number of operational and administrative details involved in running your business increases.

This chapter helps you set up procedures for running your business, choose a place to work, select furniture and equipment, buy inventory, and handle the day-to-day mundane aspects required to turn your vision into an actual business.

WHERE WILL I LOCATE MY BUSINESS?

How important is location to the success of your business? If you have a business serving a particular neighborhood or community, you have to be physically located in or near that area. If you're in retail, the choice of location may determine whether you have enough customers. If you're a manufacturer, you'll need access to raw materials and shipping, but location may otherwise not be that important. And then there are lots of companies that provide services from a distance so that external factors don't affect their choice of location at all.

Even if the site of your business doesn't seem critical, the choice of your facilities and neighborhood has an impact on how you and your employees feel about going to work. A pleasant building, in a safe neighborhood, with friendly neighbors can make work more enjoyable. It can even help in recruiting employees.

So make the choice of location carefully — it's not easily changed.

Working from Home

Many entrepreneurs know exactly where they want to work — at home! For you, I have devoted an entire chapter to setting up and working from a home office later in this Organizer. And some people run their businesses from their vehicles — cars, trucks, vans. There's information for them too in the Home Office chapter.

For everyone else, this section is for you. And even if you start out working from home, you may find you can't do it forever. I bought a house with enough room for me and my assistant to have separate offices, but as my company grew, employees soon filled the kitchen and dining room and took my desk every time I left for a meeting. Eventually, I had to have commercial office space.

Renting Space

Whether you are using your space for retail (a store), administrative (office), manufacturing (a plant), or storage purposes (a warehouse), you face many of the same considerations. The Comparison Chart and checklists on pages 119–121 can help you as you shop for space. You may also want to use the checklist as a basis for negotiating terms with your landlord.

And remember, before you sign any contract, including a lease, go over it with your lawyer first. For more on choosing a lawyer and dealing with contracts, see the next chapter entitled Legal.

One of the first decisions you need to make as you look for rental space is how you will use it. Generally, this depends on what kind of business you're in — service, retail, manufacturing, or other type.

Office Space: Virtually all businesses need at least some office space. Many businesses only need office space — professional, sales, or administrative offices. If the main purpose of your business is retail or manufacturing, your "office" may only be a small portion of your total site.

If you are a sole proprietor, just starting out, or need an additional office in another city, one solution may be to sublet space from another company or rent an "Executive Suite" office. This may provide you with a receptionist, fax, copier, Internet access, and conference room without having to set up an entire office yourself. It may also give you the flexibility of a short-term or month-to-month lease.

Retail. Location, location, location. The most important consideration for retail space is almost always the choice of location. If customers have easy access to you — either walking, driving, or taking public transportation — you have a competitive advantage over businesses that are hard to find. Also, if your business is easily seen by passers-by, you can save considerably on marketing and advertising costs. Paying higher rent to get a more visible and accessible space may be well worth it.

Manufacturing/Production. Perhaps you grow organic vegetables, produce small toys, or manufacture computer peripherals. Your product will dictate the kind of facilities you need. Your production facilities can have a direct impact on your profitability — can you work efficiently, how much energy do you consume, what are your shipping costs? Understand all costs and benefits as you choose your space.

Also consider whether you need your own facilities or whether there are contract facilities available. Some industries have contract manufacturing/production facilities (such as contract kitchens) that give you more flexibility and free up your capital, especially for those new in business.

Warehouse/Storage. Some facilities are used primarily for storage. In these situations, you have many of the same concerns as manufacturing: shipping, docks, utilities, safety, access, security, and proximity to distributors. Be particularly cautious of environmental considerations that may affect the products/materials you are storing.

Use the worksheet "Things to Consider When Renting Space" for a more detailed checklist of issues related to renting space. It includes items of general concern if you are renting space, and items specific to the type of space you are renting.

Putting Your Space to Work

Even before you select and rent a site, you should begin to design how you will use your space. This can help you determine how much space you need — you may be able to rent a smaller location or you may discover you need more space than you imagined.

LOCATION/SPACE COMPARISON CHART

	LOCATION ONE	LOCATION TWO	LOCATION THREE
Address/Contact info			
Total sq. feet			
Rent (per sq.ft., total)			
Length of lease (option to renew, at what rent?)			
What's included? (utilities, janitor, data lines?)			
What am I responsible for? (utilities, janitor, data lines?)			
Legal issues (permits, zoning, etc.)			
Parking, access, and safety issues			
Insurance issues			
Advantages			
Disadvantages			
Other			

THINGS TO CONSIDER WHEN RENTING SPACE

✔	QUESTIONS AND TERMS TO NEGOTIATE IN LEASE	NOTES
	Cost of rent: Does my rent require me also to pay the taxes, insurance, or even a percent of my income? Am I required to pay a portion of rent on "common areas"?	
	Length of lease and subletting: Can I get an option to re-new? At what rent? Can I sublet some or all of the space?	
	Layout: Does the layout of the space suit my work style or production needs? Is there lots of wasted space I pay for?	
	Leasehold improvements/remodeling: Who is responsible for improving the facility — me or the landlord? Am I responsible for returning the facility back to its original condition when I move?	
	Utilities: What utilities are included in the rent? Are adequate utilities available — electricity, water, heat?	
	Janitorial/Maintenance: Who is responsible for cleaning and repairs? Who is responsible for waste disposal?	
	Zoning laws and other use restrictions: Are there any limits on how I may make use of the premises?	
	Permits/Planning departments: What kind of permits will I need to operate my business or remodel? What are the costs and time involved?	
	Storage: Is there adequate space for storing supplies, raw materials, inventory? Is it easily accessible?	
	Safety/Security: Is the location safe for employees, customers, and my equipment and inventory?	
	Expansion: Is there sufficient space for me to grow? How soon will my needs exceed this space?	
	Environmental: What environmental limitations or concerns apply to this space? Is noise a factor — either noise I produce or noise from outside?	
	Insurance: What insurance does the owner have? What insurance must I provide? Will I have any difficulty getting adequate insurance for this location?	
	Access/Parking: Is the site easily accessible for customers, employees, shipments? Are there adequate parking spaces provided? Is it near public transportation?	
✔	**OFFICE SPACE CONSIDERATIONS**	NOTES
	Appearance: Will I be meeting clients or customers at the office and need to make a positive impression? Does the office have a waiting area?	

THINGS TO CONSIDER WHEN RENTING SPACE

✔	OFFICE SPACE CONSIDERATIONS – CONTINUED	NOTES
	Privacy: Does the office have sufficient privacy for the needs of my business?	
	Meeting space/conference rooms: Do I have sufficient access to conference rooms or other meeting space?	
	Mail shipping and receiving: Can I receive mail or shipments? Is it secure? What time does it arrive?	
	Coffee/kitchen/eating areas: Is there access to any coffee, food preparation or eating areas? Is water convenient?	
	Lighting: Does the space have adequate lighting to avoid eye strain and fatigue for me and employees?	
	Wiring/data lines: Is the space already wired for highspeed Internet access? If not, will it be difficult or expensive to install wiring?	
✔	**RETAIL SPACE CONSIDERATIONS**	NOTES
	History of others in the space: How have other retail or restaurant businesses fared at this location?	
	Fellow tenants/neighbors: Are the retail neighbors compatible, with similar market demographics?	
	Quality of the space itself: Does it feel welcoming and make it easy to show off my merchandise?	
	Limitations on space, additional fees: Are there any limits on my hours of operation, or requirements to pay additional fees or participate in certain promotions (common in malls or business improvement districts)?	
✔	**MANUFACTURING SPACE CONSIDERATIONS**	NOTES
	Docks/shipping facilities: Can I receive/ship my expected materials/inventory? Does the location incur additional shipping fees?	
	Utilities: Are there adequate utilities for my production needs — water, electricity, natural gas, etc.	
	Waste disposal: Is there adequate access and cost for waste disposal, including any hazardous materials resulting from my production process?	
	Proximity to suppliers and distributors: How long does it take to replenish materials, to send my product to distributors and customers? Costs?	
✔	**OTHER LEASE PROVISIONS?**	NOTES
	What other fees, duties, or limitations are part of the lease agreement?	

Don't forget to provide adequate space for "workstations" — copying, faxing, mail preparation/sorting, coffee/refreshments — and for storage, reception and waiting areas, and break areas for employees.

One way to design your space is to sketch a layout on a design grid, like the one provided for you on page 123. As you layout your floor plan, consider how the following might affect the way you use your space:

- **Partitions or closed offices.** How will you divide the office space or assign space to employees?
- **Private and meeting space.** How will you create adequate space for private and staff meetings?
- **Ambiance.** How will you create an atmosphere that employees will enjoy working in and enables them to work efficiently?
- **Climate control.** How will you assure that people are comfortable and equipment protected from excessive heat, cold, or moisture?

Of course, you could hire an interior decorator or ergonomics specialist to help you with your floor plan, but resist spending more money than you need to now.

Start with a preliminary layout idea, measure your square footage, and then assign each square on the grid a measurement — one foot, ten feet, etc. Grab a pencil and start scribbling. You may want to make extra copies of the grid in case you need to start over. And have fun!

More than One Location

You may find that you want or need more than one place to do business. In retail or service businesses, growth often means adding locations. If you are in manufacturing, you may find it less expensive to have your manufacturing facilities in one city and your administrative or sales offices elsewhere. Technology has also made it relatively simple to have some workers who are "remotely located," often far away from the main office.

Having more than one site presents a number of legal and logistical issues. Legal concerns range from paying sales and payroll taxes to the appropriate state to understanding insurance regulations in different states. The technology concerns of working long-distance between offices are discussed on pages 169 and 171. But don't be scared away by the concerns of having more than one location if you can save money and attract the best employees by being flexible in how and where you locate your business.

For more information on laws and regulations in different states, also consult Michael Jenkins' book *Starting and Operating a Business in the United States,* published by Running 'R' Media. It includes state-by-state information on CD-ROM.

BUYING EQUIPMENT AND FURNITURE

When you're starting or expanding a business, equipment and furniture can represent a large percent of your total costs. If you purchase or enter into a long-term lease, you will be stuck with your choices for a long time. So plan your equipment and furniture choices carefully.

Furniture

Few things make you feel like you're finally "in business" as having office furniture. If you're just starting out, getting your stuff off the dining room table and onto your own desk reinforces the sense of the seriousness of your enterprise.

When you rent offices, how your furnish your space helps set the tone and "culture" of your company and how you'll be perceived by your staff, clients, and yourself. Young, high-tech companies may be able to use inexpensive formica work tables as desks; that wouldn't work very well for a law firm.

Don't purchase your furniture until you know what space you'll be using. Sometimes you may be able to get office furniture as part of your space lease, especially in an "Executive Suite" or sublet situation. In any case, you want your furniture to fit the size and feel of the space you rent. If you expect to grow or move, look for furniture that is flexible, composed of various modules, or movable.

DESIGN GRID

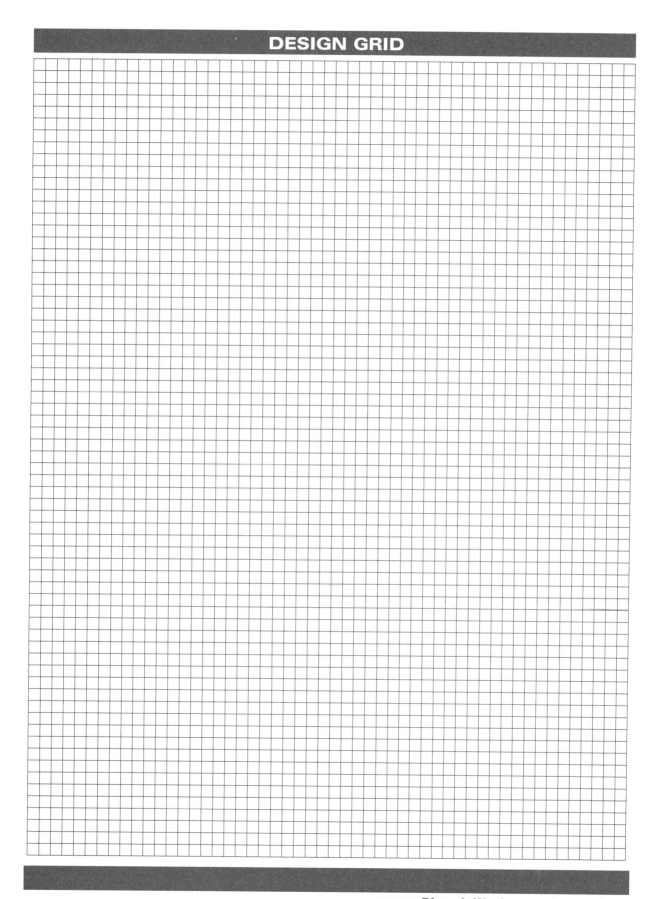

WHAT WOULD RHONDA DO . . . BUY OR LEASE

Rhonda's first rule: Buy less expensive items; lease more costly ones. It generally doesn't make much sense to lease a fax machine or printer; they're only a few hundred dollars. But if you need a major piece of equipment, don't tie up your cash.

Rhonda's second rule: The more unsure you are of your plans, the more you should lease.

Rhonda's third rule: Check the tax situation: some deductions can make leasing actually cost less than buying.

And Rhonda's most important rule: Don't get more than you need. Cash in the bank beats a nice desk chair any day.

Remember, "furniture" consists of more than just desks and chairs — you'll need storage cabinets, work tables, floor coverings, lighting, and decorative items, all of which cost money. Consider all these items as you develop your "furniture" budget. Use the Furniture Shopping List on page 126 to comparison shop and keep track of what you've ordered.

Equipment

Because a great deal of the equipment you'll need relates to technology — computers, phone systems, wireless devices — an entire chapter is devoted to Technology & Communications later in this Organizer. The section in this chapter focuses on other types of equipment.

When choosing critical business equipment, go slowly! Educate yourself about what's available. Vendors can be a great source of information and advice. If you're opening a restaurant, for instance, vendors of major appliances and equipment may be able to help you design an efficient kitchen lay-out. Industry trade shows are an outstanding time to comparison shop and become more aware of the range of options available.

Be certain you understand all the ongoing costs of owning a piece of equipment: the price and availability of supplies, the amount of specialized training necessary to operate it, vendor training and technical support available and those costs.

Begin a list now on page 127 of equipment you know you'll need, or turn to page 166 and use the equipment list in the Technology chapter. If yours is not strictly a technology company, you'll probably use both lists, one for computer-related equipment, and one for everything else!

Buying versus Leasing

As you begin shopping for furniture and equipment, you'll face the issue of whether to buy or lease. All kinds of things can be leased: furniture, equipment, vehicles, computers, telephone systems. Leasing is tempting: you'll spend less money now and perhaps won't be stuck with your choices for as long.

Some vendors, especially of expensive equipment, may offer their own financing. Ask! This may be an attractive option, as the vendor may make concessions on either the price of the equipment or on the financing costs to get your business started (and sell you continuing supplies or maintenance). Ask also whether this kind of equipment financing enables you to upgrade to newer equipment during the life of the lease/loan.

Warranties/Service Contracts

When shopping for equipment, always appraise the warranties, service contracts and technical support offered or available. A good warranty may be worth a substantial amount of money, especially if repairs are very costly. The same is true for service/maintenance contracts.

WARRANTIES AND SERVICE CONTRACTS

Equipment:
Place Purchased:
Date Purchased:
Warranty Terms:
Expiration Date:
Contact Info/Phone:

Equipment:
Place Purchased:
Date Purchased:
Warranty Terms:
Expiration Date:
Contact Info/Phone:

Equipment:
Place Purchased:
Date Purchased:
Warranty Terms:
Expiration Date:
Contact Info/Phone:

Equipment:
Place Purchased:
Date Purchased:
Warranty Terms:
Expiration Date:
Contact Info/Phone:

Equipment:
Place Purchased:
Date Purchased:
Warranty Terms:
Expiration Date:
Contact Info/Phone:

FURNITURE SHOPPING LIST

Furniture	Quantity	Cost per Item	Vendor	Date Ordered	Date to be Delivered
Desks					
Desk Chairs					
Reception Desk					
Guest/Reception Chairs					
Work/Equipment Tables					
Conference Room Tables					
Conference Room Chairs					
Bookshelves, Storage Shelves, Cabinets					
Filing Cabinets					
Lamps/Lighting					
Fire Safe/Security Storage					
White Boards					
Cubicles/Dividers					
Floor Coverings					
Decorative Items					
Other: _____ _____					

EQUIPMENT SHOPPING LIST

Equipment (List)	Cost per Quantity	Item	Date Vendor	Date to be Ordered	Delivered

WHAT WOULD RHONDA DO... TO KEEP WARRANTIES HANDY

We keep a "Warranty Notebook," with the warranties and instruction manuals of every piece of equipment and furniture we purchase. This is an effortless way to keep all warranties very handy and easy-to-find when necessary. Making a "Warranty Notebook" is simple — just take a thick (2") 3-ring binder and add plastic "sheet protectors." With each purchase, slip the warranty, all assembly directions, and any other instructions in its own sleeve (or more than one sleeve if necessary). We now have a few "Warranty Notebooks," of course, so we date them by year.

Evaluate the costs and benefits carefully, but the cost of purchasing extended warranties or service contracts is worth the peace of mind knowing that you won't be hit by an unexpected large expense if something goes wrong. If something does break down, how soon can you get the equipment repaired? If a piece of equipment is crucial for your business, every day lost while it's broken is lost income for you.

To help you keep track of your warranties and service contracts, use the worksheet on page 125.

HOW WILL I PRODUCE MY PRODUCTS/SERVICES?

Your production process will vary dramatically depending on the nature of your product. Creating hand-made crafts is far different from manufacturing high-tech electronics. But you still need a "process" — a plan for how you'll get your raw materials, the steps for turning those materials into finished goods, the labor you'll need, and how you'll ensure consistent standards and quality.

Even if what you're "producing" is a service rather than a tangible product, you'll still benefit by considering the process by which you prepare and carry out that service.

As you outline your production process, use the worksheet on page 129 to address the key issues involved. In particular, keep track of task duration and the people or organizations responsible for each step in the process.

Getting Materials and Supplies

Purchasing for your business is different from going to the mall. Your suppliers are a vital part of your company's lifeline, especially if you're in manufacturing or retail. In effect, they become your "partners." You are dependent on them to be able to go forward with your business. So when you select vendors, don't just shop on the basis of price: make certain they are reliable, can set up and maintain a shipping schedule, can respond quickly if you have unusual needs, and can work with you on terms and payment. Use the worksheet on page 130 to shop around for suppliers.

Try not to be dependent on only one or two suppliers. If you are, you'll have less flexibility on price and you'll be vulnerable if they experience problems in their business. If you have very specialized needs, you may be frustrated trying to find the supplies you require. Once again, industry trade shows and associations are a good place to begin. Remember, however, that if you have very unusual requirements, you may end up dependent on only one supplier. Instead, try to design your production to use more standard materials.

HOW WILL I GET MY PRODUCTS TO MARKET?

Even if you're the only one selling your products or services, you will probably use other parties to bring your offerings to market — distributors, wholesalers, or retailers. These intermediaries provide a variety of assistance in getting your product or service to customers, including:

DESIGNING MY PRODUCTION PROCESS

As you outline the steps involved in your production process — whether you are producing a product or a service — consider the following items, how long the steps take, and who is responsible.

What supplies do I need?
When do I need them?
How much labor is required?
How will I set standards?
How will I ensure those standards are met consistently?
How will I reduce inefficiencies in the process?
How will I ensure safety?
How will I ensure adequate access to necessary utilities?
How can I reduce waste?
How will I dispose of waste?

SUPPLIER COMPARISON CHART			
	SUPPLIER ONE	**SUPPLIER TWO**	**SUPPLIER THREE**
Name of Supplier			
Sales Rep and Contact Info			
Range of Services/ Products Offered			
Direct Costs			
Additional Costs			
Payment Terms			
Order Turn-around-time			
Shipping Costs			
Other Maintenance/ Support			
Other:			

- Their sales force
- Their reputation and relationship with customers/retailers
- Their expertise in understanding the market
- Their advertising and marketing efforts
- Their additional services for you — warehousing, shipping, packaging, etc.
- Their additional services for customers — training, support, etc.

Manufacturers in particular rely on intermediaries to get their product to market. Choosing the best distributor and retailer for your product is vital to your success.

Distributors: Few decisions directly impact your business and your finances as much as the selection of a distributor. To a large extent, they control whether or not you and your products have a fair chance to ever reach potential customers. Even if you have a terrific advertising campaign, if your distributor can't get your products on retailers' store shelves, you won't be able to make sales. And their financial practices — how long they take to pay you, how often, how they report sales, and what percentages they charge — determine your cash flow and profits.

If you are just starting out, you may feel lucky to get any distributor to represent your product, but be selective! "Shop" for distributors, and don't choose solely on the basis of how much (what percentage) they'll charge for their services. Always ask for references and check with other manufacturers that the distributor represents to see how satisfied they've been and the problems they've encountered.

If you're entering into a distribution agreement, you should absolutely get a legally-binding contract, spelling out all the various aspects of your arrangement. Hire an attorney knowledgeable about distribution agreements to review your contract — even if the distributor says it's their "standard" contract. Some of the issues to include in your agreement are covered in the worksheet on page 133.

Retailers: Your choice of retailers, too, is critical. They need to be able to attract a sufficient number of customers, promote and merchandise your products, and then pay you in a timely fashion. Don't be entranced by a big or well-known name! My first client was a sportswear manufacturer who was thrilled when he landed a major department store to carry his line. Over time, however, he discovered this store had costly requirements about how he had to package and ship his merchandise, and then always made payments very late. Even though they sold a lot of his merchandise, this store's business practices severely undermined my client's financial well-being.

If you are selling directly to retailers (instead of using a distributor to reach them) be sure you understand all the terms of your arrangement. Use the worksheet on page 132 to keep track of each retailer's specifics.

Import/Export

Many small companies overlook the concept of exporting their products or services. The Internet, of course, puts international customers right at your fingertips. But while the Internet makes it easier to connect with customers, you still have many issues before you can start shipping your beachballs to Belize.

RED TAPE ALERT!

When buying substantial business assets — furniture, equipment, hardware, vehicles — be aware of tax implications. Some assets may be deducted — "expensed" — the year bought, but the IRS places a maximum amount for any one year. After that — and for non-expensable items — you must depreciate the asset and spread the tax benefit over as many as 15 or 20 years. Assets purchased before you begin business must be depreciated, not deducted.

RETAILER COMPARISON CHART

	RETAILER ONE	RETAILER TWO	RETAILER THREE
Retailer's Name and Contact Information			
What discount schedule/price will they pay you?			
Are sales final or can unsold merchandise be returned?			
What are their packaging/shipping requirements, if any?			
Who is responsible for damaged goods?			
What are their payment terms/schedule?			
What promotions, advertising, or other sales efforts will they make?			
What "co-op" advertising or other promotions will you have to participate in?			
What charge-backs or other fees do they take?			
What is their reputation with other wholesalers?			
Other:			

DISTRIBUTOR COMPARISON CHART

When you enter into a distribution contract, here are some considerations to negotiate. Be certain to have any and all agreements reviewed by a competent attorney.

	DISTRIBUTOR ONE	DISTRIBUTOR TWO	DISTRIBUTOR THREE
Distributor Name and Contact Information			
Is the agreement exclusive or nonexclusive? What is the length of the terms, and how can either party terminate the agreement?			
What percentage do they charge? When and how often do they pay you, and what holdbacks from your payments, if any, do they make?			
What other services do they offer at what fees? What are the total fees you and the distributor are responsible for?			
Who is responsible for nonpayment by their customers?			
What minimum performance guarantees do they offer?			
What marketing efforts do they guarantee? What charges for marketing efforts do you incur or sales materials are you responsible for?			
How are damaged goods handled/paid for?			

To improve your competitiveness abroad, consider becoming certified as meeting "ISO 9000" standards. These standards were adopted by the European Commission to establish uniform quality levels, but they are increasingly necessary in trade worldwide. The ISO 9000 certification and audit process can be costly, so carefully weigh the necessity and benefits of certification. More information can be found online at the International Organization for Standardization, www.iso.ch.

The U.S. Government has a number of programs to assist and encourage American companies in exporting. A wealth of information can be found on the Internet. Start at TradeNet, www.tradenet.gov. to find local trade service centers, resources, and Small Business Development Center counselors in your area.

Also check out the Trade Information Center of the Department of Commerce, www.trade.gov/td/tic. This has information about individual countries, industries, and international trade shows. Another useful source is the International Trade Administration at www.trade.gov.

The worksheet on page 135 can help you target particular markets and outline your exporting issues.

MANAGING DAILY OPERATIONS

Once your business is up and running, you're quickly going to find yourself with too much to do and too little time to do it. What inevitably happens is that many things start to fall through the cracks.

One way to help prevent this is by setting up systems to help you keep track of all the many tasks and administrative details you have to take care of. Even the smallest companies should put in place systems to handle:

- Calendar/schedules
- Mail opening and processing
- Bill paying
- Getting invoices out
- Tax deadlines
- Tracking customers' orders and accounts
- Personnel files, including tracking employees' hours, vacations, time-off, etc.
- "To do" lists

In addition to having a personal organizer or calendar, a good way to keep reminders of important and pending matters is to set up a "tickler" system to remind you each day of the things you have to do.

One type of physical "tickler" system is a tickler file. Set up 12 file folders, one for each month, and a set numbered 1 through 31 for each day of the month. Put matters that have to be handled in a particular month in the folder corresponding to that month, and on the first day of each month, put those things you have to deal with on particular days in the file folder corresponding to that date. Get in the habit of checking the daily folder each morning to see what you must do that day.

You can also use a computer program to track your "to do" lists, or you can use the "Rhonda's Reminders" system at www.RhondaWorks.com to track your tasks and get daily reminders of your "to do" list.

Increasingly, you can do many other administrative tasks on the Internet. There are a variety of helpful applications — ASPs, or application service providers — that enable you to handle many day-to-day matters from any computer that has access to the Internet.

INSURANCE: WHAT TO GET AND WHEN

One of the most frustrating expenses you'll incur is that of insurance. After all, you can't "see" what you're getting. If you're new to business, you'll be absolutely overwhelmed by the number of different types of insurance you'll need or want.

Figuring out your insurance coverage will be daunting. Guaranteed! So you'll need a good insurance agent, or two or three! Ideally, you'll find an agent

EXPORT MARKETS COMPARISON CHART

	MARKET ONE	MARKET TWO	MARKET THREE
Where are the best international markets for my product?			
What strategies will I use to develop this market? (e.g., Internet, trade shows, agent, licensing)			
How will I communicate with and serve customers in this market?			
What benefits do I expect from exporting to this market?			
What financial and human resources are required to serve this market?			
How do the following apply in this market: Tariffs/duties/taxes			
Shipping			
Customs			
Currency Conversion			
Financing/Collection			
Foreign regulations			
U.S. export regulations			
Language/cultural differences			
Dispute resolution			
Other:			

WHAT WOULD RHONDA DO. . . TO MANAGE PAYROLL

Soon after I hired my first full-time employee, I started using a payroll service. Determining payroll deductions and depositing payroll taxes with the proper authorities can be time-consuming and exacting. Moreover, the penalties for being late or getting things wrong can be substantial. It's much easier — and safer — to hire a professional service to take care of the administrative details of payroll for you.

A payroll service charges a modest amount, based on the number of employees, and how many states your employees are located in, but you're likely to easily save at least this amount in terms of your own administrative staff time, bookkeeper or accountant's help, and any penalties you may incur for late or inaccurate payments.

who understands business insurance for companies of your size and industry. It's best if they're a "broker" who can offer you policies from a number of different companies rather than just representing one insurance company's products. And you'll want someone whose advice you can trust, because you are likely going to rely on their recommendations for the type and amount of coverage you should have.

Some insurance may be required by others — such as landlords or lenders who require fire and damage insurance, or the government which requires you to have worker's compensation insurance.

Certain types of insurance are typical employee benefits — such as health, dental, life or disability insurance. Other insurance protects you from lawsuits — such as malpractice or liability insurance — and other insurance protects you from major loss in case of disasters, fire, flood, earthquake, or business interruption.

Deciding what types and how much insurance to carry is always a juggling act. You want to have enough to cover you in case of problems, but the costs can be discouraging, especially for a young company. Use the worksheet on page 137 to help you plan and compare your insurance needs.

Summary

How you handle the day-to-day operations and administration of your company directly affects your success. While these details may seem mundane, in fact, they may make all the difference in whether you are profitable, have sufficient cash flow to pay your bills, or stay out of trouble with authorities. The wrong location can doom a retail business, a poor manufacturing process can result in higher costs, lower quality, or too much waste. These issues are so important you may want to develop a detailed Operations Plan or manual to outline your processes in greater detail.

COMPARISON CHART FOR INSURANCE COVERAGE

	OPTION 1	OPTION 2	OPTION 3
Health			
Dental			
Vision			
Life/Disability			
Worker's Compensation			
Fire			
Loss/Theft			
Business Interruption			
Malpractice (errors & omissions)			
Vehicles			
Unemployment			
Offsite equipment			
Offsite employees			
Other:			
Other:			

MY WILD IDEAS

Wild Ideas for Operations:

Wild Ideas for Administration:

legal

Taking care of your company's legal health is like taking care of your personal health: an ounce of prevention is much more pleasant than a pound of cure. Time after time, I see entrepreneurs end up in legal battles costing thousands of dollars that could have been avoided with a $200 trip to an attorney.

Make your first visit to a lawyer right at the beginning of your business life. When I started my consulting practice, I spent two hours with a lawyer. We not only wrote a simple letter-of-agreement I could use with clients, but we also discussed how to price my services, collect overdue fees, and minimize taxes.

The best way to find a lawyer is by asking for referrals, especially from others in your industry. It's always better, and cheaper in the long run, to get an attorney who has experience with your type of business. Make sure you use a business lawyer; don't just turn to the "great" lawyer who handled your friend's divorce.

Most lawyers charge by the hour, but some have set fees for specific tasks, such as incorporation. Don't

hesitate to interview your prospective lawyer and ask about costs before engaging their services. You have the right to choose someone you're comfortable with and can afford.

In addition to making that vital trip to a lawyer's office, you can also consult a number of excellent legal resources on the web and in books. One of the best is Nolo.com. Nolo's website, www.nolo.com, provides a wealth of free information, and their legal books and software are first-rate. Even if you're planning to see a lawyer, I'd recommend you look around Nolo's site before your appointment to better understand what questions to ask.

But don't depend on do-it-yourself law. Establish a good working relationship with a business attorney and become used to consulting with them before you make any major business decisions.

> ## Rhonda's Rule
> ### get to know a lawyer —
> ### even before you start
> ### your business

WHAT LEGAL FORM WILL MY COMPANY TAKE?

One of the first questions you'll face when setting up your business is what "legal form" it should be. This sounds like it's purely a legal question, but it actually determines who owns your company, how it's governed, and how it will be treated by taxing authorities.

QUESTIONS TO ASK . . . A LAWYER

- What is your specialty or particular area of expertise?
- Have you ever worked with businesses in my industry before?
- Do you have any clients who are in similar businesses? Competing businesses?
- Is there any reason you'd have a conflict of interest representing me?
- What is your workload like? Are you generally available when clients call?
- Will I be working with you or with an associate or other attorney?
- How much do you charge per hour? How do you charge for additional expenses (pass-through, add on a percentage, etc.)? How much do you charge for the services of associates or paralegals?

Sole Proprietorship. Most of us begin as "sole proprietors" — just us and our business. This is the simplest and least expensive arrangement. But if you want to grow — have partners, secure investors, add employees, incur substantial liabilities — you should examine other corporate legal forms and discuss the pros and cons of each with a competent attorney.

Partnership. A partnership can be a simple arrangement, with all parties actively engaged in running the business and sharing liabilities. If others are willing to invest in your company but won't be actively engaged in management, you can form a "Limited Partnership" so they limit their financial exposure to just the amount they're investing and not to taking on the debts of the company.

Corporation. A corporation is considered by federal and state law to be its own legal entity — corporations can enter into contracts, be sued, hire employees, etc. As such, the corporation itself (and not the owners) incurs the business' debts and assumes the liabilities, providing a layer of legal and financial protection for the individual owners and their personal assets. Being a corporation doesn't provide complete protection for company owners, especially for tax avoidance, but it gives them limited liability, and that's one of the greatest attractions of incorporating.

Limited Liability Company (LLC). An LLC gives you many of the same benefits as a corporation,

without formally incorporating. But there are some limits on LLCs.

When considering which legal form to choose for your business, carefully consider the pros and cons of each type; the effect on ownership, governance and taxes; and, of course, consult a lawyer!

For more details on incorporation and LLCs, also consult Michael Jenkins' invaluable resource for small business startups, *Starting and Operating a Business in the United States.*

A brief summary of the different types of legal entities is included on pages 142–143.

Get Everything In Writing

Sears and Roebuck, Hewlett and Packard, Ben and Jerry. Great partnerships often make great companies. The way most people go into business with others is by taking on partners. They might not use the term "partner" immediately, but if you and a friend decide to start selling used golf balls on the Internet together, in the eyes of the law, you've become partners.

If you're going into business with other people, even just a spouse or friend, formalize your arrangement with a partnership agreement. Partnerships can be terrific, but they can often be stressful, and when things go wrong between the partners, it can mean the demise of the whole company. So take time to

DISCUSSING PARTNERSHIP TERMS

Use this worksheet to determine with your partners the terms of your partnership. Then meet with a lawyer to draw up a formal agreement.

Ownership Division. Who owns what percent?

Jobs/Responsibilities. What jobs and responsibilities does each partner have? Can partners work for any other company or do any other work on the side?

Decisions. How will general business decisions be made? What decisions does each partner have final authority on? Who has the final authority for decisions for the company as a whole?

Communication. How will you communicate on a regular basis? How will serious disputes be resolved?

Exit Strategy and Dissolution Agreement. What happens if one partner wants to leave the business or move? What if one partner wants to sell the company? What happens if a partner dies or becomes disabled?

Other:

FORMS OF BUSINESS ORGANIZATION COMPARED

Legal Form	What Is It?	Advantages?
Sole Proprietorship	A business owned by one person that is not incorporated or an LLC. If you don't set up any other legal structure, and no one else owns any part of your business, you have a sole proprietorship.	Simple. No legal forms or costs to establish. No "double taxation."
General Partnership	A business with more than one owner in which all partners actively participate in the business.	You have the time and talents of more than one person. No double taxation.
Limited Partnership	A business with at least one owner who manages the business (general partners) and other partners who do not participate in the management (limited partners).	Protects the personal assets of limited partners, who are not responsible for the debts and obligations of the business. Enables investors to limit their financial exposure.
Limited Liability Company (LLC) or Limited Liability Partnership	A legal form which provides much of the protection of incorporating with most of the simplicity of a sole proprietorship.	Protects your personal assets against most business losses. No double taxation. Relatively simple, inexpensive to establish and maintain. Can distribute profits and losses disproportionately to ownership interest.
C Corporation	A corporation is a legal entity, separate from its owners.	Protects owners' personal assets against corporate losses and obligations. Can issue stock. No limit on the number of people who can own stock. Can deduct cost of benefits for all employees, including owners.
S Corporation	A type of corporation that allows for pass-through taxation instead of double taxation. S corporations are less popular since the introduction of LLCs.	The personal liability protection of a corporation with the pass-through taxation treatment of a sole proprietorship.

FORMS OF BUSINESS ORGANIZATION COMPARED

Disadvantages?	Tax Treatment	Watch Out For
Provides no protection of personal assets from business losses. The business owner has unlimited personal liability for the debts, obligations, and judgments against the company. The business owner's spouse may likewise be liable.	"Pass through" profits and losses, so the business owner can deduct losses against other personal income, and there is no "double taxation." File a Schedule C with your income tax return.	In community property states, spouses may be liable for business debts as well as having an ownership interest in the company.
Each partner has unlimited personal liability for business losses or obligations. Each partner can sign contracts and incur debts that all partners are liable for.	"Pass through" profits and losses to the partners who pay tax at their individual rates. Partnership pays no taxes but must file a Form 1065.	If you go into business with other people, you have a partnership whether you draw up documents or not, and they will have a share of the business and other legal rights.
Limited partners cannot participate in running the company. General partners are all liable for the company's obligations.	Limited partners can only deduct "passive" losses against "passive income," and they are capped on the total amount of their investment.	If a limited partner participates in any way in the management of the company, they can lose their liability protection.
Each owner can enter into contracts and incur debts for the entire LLC. Must file Articles of Organization with your state; often requires filing and annual state fees.	"Pass through" profits and losses to each owner. LLC pays no taxes but must file a Form 1065.	Be sure to have a written agreement spelling out the percentage ownership of each member to avoid confusion or conflict later.
Double taxation. Must file articles of incorporation with your state; requires filing and annual state fees. Must keep records and have an annual meeting. Requires board of directors in most states if more than one stockholder.	Double taxation: corporation and shareholders each pay tax on income they receive. However, if the corporation will keep significant amounts in reserve, this can have lower tax consequences than pass-through taxation.	Securities rules affect how you sell stock and to whom. Use lawyers to set up a corporation.
Many disadvantages over an LLC, including limits on number and residency of stockholders, requires proportionate distribution of profits and losses, more record keeping required than an LLC.	"Pass through" taxation, but profits and losses must be allocated on same percentage as ownership.	Ask your lawyer if there is any benefit in choosing an S corporation over an LLC.

work out as many details as you can when you first enter into a partnership with anyone. The worksheet on page 141 is a good beginning for a discussion with a partner, outlining important issues that can later become part of a formal agreement, drawn up with the help of a lawyer.

Who Owns My Business?

One of the key issues involved in choosing a legal form for your business is determining who owns it. In a sole proprietorship, you own it. In any other form, you share ownership, either with a partner or shareholders.

If you're brand new to business, you may imagine that you can get someone to invest in your company but leave you completely alone. Wouldn't that be nice! The truth is, the minute someone owns a piece of your company, they acquire certain rights and, if you didn't set up a corporation, LLC, or limited partnership to limit investors' personal liability, they may also become responsible for the business' debts.

You may also think you're protected from other "owners" meddling as long as you keep more than 50% ownership in the company. But, depending on the corporate form, whether you have a board of directors, the U.S. state your company is in, and other factors, shareholders not only have rights; they can actually make binding decisions for the company, even removing you from management. Before you begin parting with any ownership interest in

your company, consult a knowledgeable attorney (and possibly an accountant as well).

Issuing Stock

Corporations are the only entities that can issue stock, and they can issue different classes of stock, with some shareholders getting preferential treatment (as in the dividing of corporate assets in the event of a dissolution of the corporation). Being able to issue stock is invaluable in attracting investors and employees.

In the early days of your business, you may be tempted to promise or hand out stock to anyone who'll give you money or provide services. After all, you've got a lot more stock than cash. The fact that others want stock in your business is a sign of their faith in your ability to make that stock worth something one day.

But anytime you issue stock, you not only have legal and financial considerations; you're also diluting your own ownership of the company. When you give someone stock, they're getting a "share" of the company and a percentage of the ownership.

So before you start making promises, sit down and come up with a "Stock Distribution Plan." Investors, of course, will take a significant piece of the ownership, as will any other company founders. If you need to recruit other key employees (such as a CEO or chief technology officer), they'll want to get a fairly large amount of stock also. Set aside a pool of stock for all other employees. You may also be

RED TAPE ALERT!

The best way for things to stay friendly between partners is to have a clearly defined partnership agreement BEFORE you begin the company. Prepare a legally-binding contract spelling out the terms of your partnership: who owns what percent, how decisions are made, what happens to the company if one or more of the partners wishes to leave, how and whether additional partners can be added, etc. It is also advisable to work out a "Buy/Sell" agreement, so the terms of how and to whom a partner can leave or sell their interest in the business are clear. You may want provisions limiting their ability to sell their interest to others and, in the case of a partner's death or disability, to have other partners buy out their heirs at a fair price — you don't necessarily want to be running the business with your partners' spouse or child.

RED TAPE ALERT!

Any time you deal with stock in your company, you face a host of potential legal and tax implications. Be very cautious about distributing or promising stock in your company, and don't do it before you've discussed it thoroughly with a competent attorney and accountant! If, for instance, in the early days of your company, you give a consultant a certain amount of stock in return for a certain monetary value of service (e.g., 10,000 shares of stock for $5,000 worth of graphic design work), you may inadvertently be placing a value on all other stock that the company has issued or will issue, including the stock you and other founders own, which may have a significant tax impact on you and others. If you are issuing stock to company founders, or stock options to employees, be sure the correct paperwork, including a "Form 83B Election," has been done, or you may all incur significantly higher taxes.

required or want to give stock to consultants or other service providers, as well as granting stock to your advisory committee members, strategic partners, and others.

Establishing a stock option or stock purchase plan for all employees can be highly motivating, as your employees feel a sense of participation in the overall growth of the company.

You'll also have to decide when a person's stock "vests" or becomes theirs. Because you want to encourage employees to remain with the business, you typically want to require the stock to vest over a period of years. If you set up a four-year vesting period, for example, employees might be entitled to one-fourth of their stock after the first year, and then "earn" another 1/48th of their stock each month (4 years times 12 months).

Use the worksheets on pages 146–147 to outline your stock distribution plan.

HOW DO I PROTECT MY INTELLECTUAL PROPERTY?

What is the value of the Nike "swoosh?" The design of a Macintosh computer? The content of a Beatles song? We all recognize that these things have a value far beyond the "physical property" of the running shoes, computers, or CDs themselves because of the "intellectual property" of the swoosh, the design, or the wonderful music and lyrics of John Lennon and Paul McCartney.

Every company has certain intangible things that are, or can be, very valuable. Many of these come under the heading of "Intellectual Property" — assets that have value because of the knowledge, recognition, inventiveness, etc. that they consist of. Indeed, some companies ONLY have products composed of intellectual property — software developers, writers, inventors, consultants, and many more.

So just as you would protect the physical property of your company, you need to protect your intellectual property.

Trade Secrets. Just about every company has ideas or knowledge that gives them a competitive edge, and which would be harmful if shared with others. If you're just starting out, your business concept may be one of your major assets. But "trade secrets" covers a huge range of things — from how you make a product, to the preferences of your best customer. The law provides a certain amount of protection to you for your trade secrets — but only if you take steps to keep such information secret. So be careful how you disseminate information: mark documents "confidential," get others to sign NonDisclosure agreements, put passwords and other security measures on "work-in-progress" websites or computer programs, and be careful who you talk to!

STOCK DISTRIBUTION PLAN

What percentage of the company do you want or need to give to others? In a young company, the number of shares is not as important as the percentage ownership those shares represent. Use this worksheet to plan the distribution of stock in your company.

	# of Shares	% Ownership	Vesting Period
Founder #1			
Founder# 2			
Founder #3			
CEO			
Chief Operating Officer			
Chief Technology Officer			
Chief Financial Officer			
Other Officer level employees			
VP level employees			
Director level employees			
Manager level employees			
Other long-time or key employees			
Other employee levels			
Investors			
Consultants/Professional Service firms			
Advisory Committee Members			
Board of Director Members			
Strategic Partners			
Others			

PEOPLE YOU'VE GIVEN OR PROMISED STOCK

Use this space to keep track of people to whom you've given or promised stock. When starting a new company, you may use promises of stock in many ways — from raising venture money to getting your logo designed. Discuss with your lawyer how to draw up these formal agreements.

Name	Amount or Value of Stock

RED TAPE ALERT!

Whenever you have others help create any of your intellectual property, you want to make clear who owns what they develop. For instance, if you have a graphic designer create your logo, software developers write computer code, or writers create content, who owns the rights to all those creations? In most cases, you want to make sure you do! So in your contract or agreement, clarify the ownership of the work product, make certain that they are required to transfer any copyright or other ownership if necessary, and specify that you are hiring them on a "Work for Hire" basis, with all work product becoming your property. And have the agreement looked at by an attorney.

NonDisclosure Agreements: One of the simplest ways to protect your ideas is to get a signed NonDisclosure agreement or confidentiality agreement before discussing your concepts with others. This is a typical procedure, and you'll often be asked to sign NDAs if you're trying to do business with another company. Venture capitalists will NOT sign NDAs, as they see too many new business ideas.

NonCompete Agreements: Once a trade secret is learned, it can't be unlearned. So sometimes the biggest fear you have is that a valuable and knowledgeable employee will go to work for a competitor. To help guard against this, you may want to have employees sign an agreement limiting their ability to go work for a competing company (or start their own competing company) for a period of time. NonCompete agreements provide a measure of protection, but courts don't like enforcing them, so make certain they are carefully written and appropriately used. Some states, like California, may not enforce NonCompete agreements.

but it gives local authorities information on what kinds of businesses are being operated in their community and who is responsible for the company. Of course, there are usually fees or taxes they collect too! Cities frequently require other permits to operate certain kinds of businesses, install certain business equipment, or make changes to facilities.

You may also need licenses from the state or other authorities to operate certain businesses. States regulate many kinds of industries, from barbershops to liquor stores to contractors. In a few cases, you may even need to get federal licenses (such as interstate moving). This may all seem overwhelming. Check with www.Rhondaworks.com, ask your attorney, or consult with a local Small Business Development Counselor about the licenses you'll need in your community and for your type of business.

Use the worksheet on page 149 to keep track of the business licenses and permits you need.

DO I NEED A BUSINESS LICENSE?

Whoa! You may be ready to start or expand your business, but the authorities may not want you to — at least not without making sure you have the proper licenses or permits. As frustrating as it may seem, you can't just rent an office or a store and set up shop.

Most cities or counties require some form of basic business license. This may feel like "Big Brother,"

TRADEMARKS/ SERVICE MARKS

You're thrilled! You've picked the perfect name for your new breakfast cereal company: "Yummy Tummy." You've even invented a cartoon character, "Yummy Tummy Tillie," to symbolize your brand. You're ready to set the world on fire!

Not so fast. Before you start making "Yummy Tummy" a household name, you need to make sure you can use and protect the name. You don't want to invest

BUSINESS LICENSES & PERMITS

List the licenses and permits you need, including where and how to apply, requirements and fees.

LICENSE TYPE	AGENCY & CONTACT INFO	REQUIREMENTS	FEES
Local Licenses:			
Local Permits:			
County Licenses/ Permits:			
State Licenses:			
DBA required:			
Federal certification:			
Other:			

money and time building "brand equity" — value associated with the name of your company — just to discover someone else is already using "Yummy Tummy."

That's where trademark laws come in. Trademark laws protect owners of a company from other companies using their names, logos, taglines, or other distinctive marks on similar or competing products or services.

When you apply for a trademark (or a servicemark, for marks that refer to a company or service rather than a product), you indicate what category or categories of products or services you'll use it for; you don't "own" the name in all instances. If you're using "Yummy Tummy" for breakfast cereal, someone else could get the rights to use the same name for unrelated products or services — a weight-reduction program, for instance.

There are, of course, limits to what you can trademark, and it's often frustrating to find that the simplest names aren't able to be trademarked, as a name has to be "distinctive" and not simply "descriptive." For instance, you can't get a trademark for a health resort merely called "Spa," because it's too descriptive. But you could for a body oil of the same name. Once the Internet is involved, things get even stickier. Legal names that include "dot com" can be trademarked, such as "Spa.com."

In fact, if you're inventing a whole new product category, you may need to come up with a generic way to describe the generic term, in order to trademark your chosen name. My client, Patrick McConnell,

invented what he called the MountainBoard.™ To get that name trademarked, Patrick had to come up with the term "all terrain board" to avoid his brand name being viewed as merely descriptive.

To get started on your name and trademark search, begin at the U.S. Patent and Trademark Office online search (www.uspto.gov — look at searchable databases) and also go to the "whois" section of Network Solutions (www.networksolutions.com). This is only a first-level trademark search, however. Consider hiring a trademark attorney for a more complete search.

Protecting your name online. The Internet makes trademark issues really baffling. You may have happily and legally been doing business in one state for decades without being confused with a business using the same name in another state. Now one of you puts up a site on the Internet, and customers don't know who's who.

In the early days, cybersquatters would take www.nameofbigcompany.com and demand large sums of money to give it to the trademark owner. Now such cybersquatters can legally be forced to give up trademarked names — except if they have any legitimate use. Since many companies can have the same trademark name in different categories, your domain name may legally be taken by another trademark owner without you having any recourse.

Copyrights. If you're creating works that others might want to copy — content, music, art, software, illustrations, etc. — you'll want to protect what you've created. This is where copyright law comes in.

WHAT WOULD RHONDA DO . . . ABOUT TRADEMARKS

Avoid any name close to or potentially confusing with a big company's trademark. It may seem silly when a big corporation goes after a tiny company, but if a company doesn't protect their trademark, the law says they can lose it. They have no choice but to sue. Even if you're legally in the clear, with a trademark issued to you, the reality is that in trademark issues, the side with the greatest ability and willingness to spend money on lawyers gets their way. McDonald's, for instance, vigorously goes after any company that uses the prefix "Mc" even for products or services that could not possibly be confused with food. So don't even think of naming your barber shop "McHaircut."

TRADEMARK SEARCH RESULTS

As you consider various names, taglines, and logos for your business, look to see whether any other companies have already trademarked competing or similar marks.

Name/Tagline/Mark	Others Using It/Similar?	What Category?

Copyrights cover any kind of work that is "fixed" and "tangible" — even if it's only computer code, words spoken on an audio tape, or images "fixed" on a movie.

Copyrights do not cover "ideas," no matter how novel, just the particular fixed expression of that idea. So you can't copyright your idea to have a boy go off to a school for wizards, but you can copyright your novel telling the story of this boy. Once you have a copyright, you retain the rights to that creation, and no one else can make a movie about your hero without your permission. And you also can't copyright "facts." So if what you're creating is purely the compilation of facts, you won't be able to copyright that.

Copyrights are easy to get. The rights to your creation are yours when you create it; theoretically, you don't have to do anything to insure your copyright. But that's putting you at some risk. The easiest thing to do to protect your copyright is to add a simple copyright notice whenever you produce something. Just add the word "copyright," the © notice, the date, and your name. (This book is copyright © 2001, Rhonda Abrams.) For further protection, and to make certain there is no dispute as to when it was created, you can register your copyright inexpensively in the U.S. with the U.S. Copyright Office (www.loc.gov/copyright).

Patents. Copyrights are easy to get; patents are incredibly tough. Copyrights are free; patents are incredibly expensive. Copyrights are yours the instant you create the work; patents can take years to get issued. Patents are also difficult and costly to enforce. So if you're building your business around a new invention, process, machine, recipe, or formula that needs to be patented, it's going to be tough going.

If, however, you have a new invention or a new process that is indeed unique, "non-obvious" (a requirement for qualifying for a patent), and worth a lot of money, then pursue the patent process. The first thing you'll need — after you've come up with your new invention or idea — is a good patent attorney. A good one will warn you of the costs and pitfalls before you get too far down the road.

OTHER LEGAL AGREEMENTS

Remember, I told you at the beginning of this chapter you need to become well-acquainted with a competent attorney? Well, I meant it, because once you're in business, you'll have a wide-range of legal documents and agreements you'll enter into. And it's a good idea to have an attorney you can turn to who understands your business.

If you'll be entering into the same kinds of agreements repeatedly — for instance, a letter of engagement for your consulting services — have an attorney help you draft a standard template into which you can just plug the specifics each time.

Some of the many types of legal agreements you may need include:

- Letter of Engagement (for your services)
- Letter of Intent (for strategic partnerships, customers, etc.)
- Distribution Agreement
- Leases
- Independent Contractor Agreement

Follow through and get the agreements signed. Don't rely on a verbal agreement — get everything in writing.

Summary

If you do nothing else after reading this chapter, consult with an attorney. Once you're in business, you face all kinds of legal concerns and issues. Get your agreements and contracts signed, both to avoid misunderstandings and to protect yourself if something goes wrong. While the days of doing business with just a handshake may not be over entirely, doing so leaves you at risk. Ours is a litigious society, and the best way to avoid ending up in court — or in hot water — is to see an attorney long before the problems start.

VITAL STATISTICS

Use this worksheet to keep track of those important dates, numbers and information about the legal status of your business or yourself. You may be asked to refer to these often.

Date of Incorporation:
Corporation Number:
Formal Company Name:
"dbas"/in what county filed/date/numbers:
Federal Employer Identification Number ("EIN"):
State Employer Identification Number:
Business License or Permit/Number:
Business License or Permit/Number:
Business License or Permit/Number:
Better Business Bureau Number:
Unemployment Insurance Provider/ Date of Instatement, Renewal Date:
Other:

MY (NOT SO) WILD IDEAS ABOUT LEGAL MATTERS

technology & communication

"Do you have a website?" "Send me an e-mail with the details." "Let me fax it over."

In today's world, technology and communication are wound up together. Whether we work globally or locally, most of the ways we stay in touch with others is by using technology — phones, e-mail, the Internet, fax machines, wireless devices.

This chapter focuses on the communication and technology issues facing every business. The next chapter — "e-business" — provides additional information and worksheets for those who have a company that is actually conducting transactions — making sales — on the Internet.

A COMMUNICATION PLAN

People in business find it hard to stay in touch. There's always work to be done, so why spend the time just talking? But that's where problems arise. Frustrated employees don't know what's happening in their company, customers can't get calls returned, suppliers don't understand why a payment is late. In fact, lack of client communication is the number one complaint received by bar associations about attorneys.

It's also all-too-easy to be inconsistent in our communication, telling people something one day and then doing something differently the next. We may know that circumstances have changed, but when we forget to let others know, it makes them discouraged or angry.

None of us are going to perfect our communication skills, but there are a number of steps we can take to improve them. First, fill out the "Communication Plan" worksheet on page 157. Next, keep the following tips in mind:

- **Explain.** Be sure everyone involved in a project understands, from the beginning, as much as possible about the nature of the work, the overall goals, the timetable, and the possible complications or delays.

- **Stay in touch.** Let people know what you're doing, or find out how they're doing. If you're working for a client, keep them informed — even if the task isn't done. With employees, don't "hover," but don't let them think they can't ask you questions either.

- **Let people know.** Whenever anything happens that alters original plans or previous decisions, let people know as soon as possible. Things happen. Plans change. Problems arise. Others will be much less frustrated if they're told of changes right away.

- **Acknowledge.** Don't wait for a project to be finished or for success to be achieved to acknowledge other people's efforts. Let people know they're doing a good job while they're still doing it.

- **Listen.** Listening is an absolutely critical business skill, particularly for those in management or sales. My first year in business, I lost a potentially large customer because when they asked me what I did, I immediately began to tell them. Instead, I should have started a dialogue, listening to why they had called me and what their needs were.

When people in business want to know how to communicate better, what they usually mean is they want to know how to persuade others to see and do things their way. They focus on what they're going to say. But don't underestimate the importance of listening. When you think about developing your communication plan, also consider how to improve your listening skills. Listening doesn't mean just giving another person a chance to speak; it means actively listening to what they're saying, asking questions, and reflecting on what they've said.

"No Tech" or "Low Tech" Communication

Most of this chapter concentrates on using technology to improve communication, but remember, people were communicating with one another before the first telephone was ever invented. No technology device has ever improved on the amount of information and the quality of the interaction we can get from actually being face-to-face with another human being. So, as you plan your communication, also consider the no-tech or low-tech ways to stay in touch.

Face-to-face meetings: These can be as complicated as traveling across country to meet with a client, or as simple as stopping by someone's desk to chat for a few minutes. But "face time" is crucial — with customers, employees, referral sources. If you regularly work at a distance from someone, plan time to interact in-person and keep the relationship fresh and deep.

Staff Meetings: Everybody hates meetings! They seem an inefficient way to get things done and to spend time. But staff meetings actually can be a relatively good way to communicate, share, and come to group decisions. It's difficult to find a balance between too many meetings and too few, but typically small and growing companies are less likely to have sufficient meetings to keep everyone abreast of rapidly-changing developments.

Picking up the phone: One of the easiest and best ways to stay in touch with someone is to give them a phone call. The downside, of course, is you can play "telephone tag," and that's why e-mail is such an efficient replacement. But e-mail often leaves room to be misunderstood. You can build a stronger relationship with someone when you can hear each other's voices.

COMMUNICATION TOOLS

You never have to be out of touch. There are a profusion of devices to keep you connected and new ones are being introduced every day. Since many of these are so new, expect to see many changes in the

WHAT WOULD RHONDA DO: HAND WRITTEN NOTES

In a world where everything is produced on a computer, you'd be surprised at the strength of a hand-written note. I keep note cards handy to send hand-written thank you notes. I travel with these notecards, too, so I can write notes on the plane home after I've met with new clients or contacts. Don't fret too much over what to say; keep it simple: "I just wanted to let you know I enjoyed our first meeting, and I look forward to working with you," or "Thank you for your referral. I appreciate it."

MY COMMUNICATION PLAN

Who do I need to stay in touch with?	How often?	How will I communicate with them?	What do they need to know?
Customers			
Potential customers			
Past customers			
Employees			
Contractors			
Sales reps			
Suppliers			
Distributors			
Funding sources			
Industry colleagues			
Referral sources			
Others:			

types of services you have available, the providers who offer them, the cost, equipment, etc. Because you can anticipate so many changes, be cautious as you purchase these. Don't become completely dependent on a device that may become outdated or a provider that may stop service.

Choosing a Phone System

The telephone is our single most important piece of business communication equipment. Even in this day of high-tech devices, your phone system is your life-line to the world.

In comparison to other forms of business communication, phone lines and phone calls are inexpensive. Compare the cost of your monthly phone calls to the cost of printing and mailing even one brochure. Being cheap with your phones may actually cost you money. I knew one man who exported goods from the U.S. to South America. He boasted to me that he didn't have an answering machine or voice mail. "That way they have to call me, and I never have to return expensive long-distance calls." Right, but even one missed deal may have cost him more than a year's worth of phone calls.

Another typical scenario is the entrepreneur who spends months searching for the right office and a bundle on a computer system, and then, at the last minute, has their secretary call the phone company to install the phones. Missed calls, lost messages, and an inefficient phone system are the likely result.

Instead, spend time setting up phone service with your local or long-distance carrier, keeping these pointers in mind:

> ### *Rhonda's Rule*
> **use your phone . . . a lot!**

- **Develop a plan.** Start by sitting down and planning your phone service, just as you would any other important aspect of your business. How do you use your phones now or anticipate using them? What features must you have? Which would you like? What frustrates you or your customers about your current phone service?

- **Consider special features.** Phone companies offer many enhancements to your basic phone services. Investigate ways your phone can be a powerful business tool.

- **Keep it simple.** On the other hand, if your phones are too complicated, they'll be a nuisance to use. Don't buy "bells and whistles" that will get in the way of using your phone as a phone.

- **Comparison shop.** The features and costs of phone service and equipment vary widely. Shop around for long-distance plans and other services to find the right fit for your business.

- **Think long term.** Will you be expanding, moving, changing your needs? If so, either buy a scalable and changeable system, or buy an inexpensive system that you can replace without a large financial loss.

- **Enable customers to reach a real person.** When you're setting up a voice mail system, avoid "voice mail purgatory," where callers can never reach a real human being. Never make a person go through more than three steps to reach the person, voice mail, or automated service they called for.

WHAT WOULD RHONDA DO: SERVING ANOTHER LOCATION

Want a presence in another city but don't have money to open and staff a second office? With a remote location number, you can get a local phone number and also a listing in the local phone book, and all calls are immediately forwarded to your regular phone number. Voila! You can serve another community even though you don't have an office or even a phone instrument there. You pay a small monthly fee plus toll calls, if any. This is also a good idea if you're moving; you can keep a presence — and customers — in your former city.

MY PHONE NEEDS

	How Many?	Service Provider?	Special Features?
Voice lines			
Fax/data lines			
Voice mail boxes			
Long distance service			
Cell phones			
White Pages and Yellow Pages listings			
Other:			

Who is your local service provider? Do you have a choice in provider? _____
_____

Will you have phone numbers in remote locations? Where should they ring? _____
_____

How will you receive and direct incoming calls? Will you have a receptionist, or an automated system? _____
_____

What types of on-hold features do you need? How can you transfer calls between phone lines?
_____

Do you want or need caller ID, and how much does it cost? _____

Can you integrate your phone system with your database or other software? How can integration better serve your business? _____
_____

Can you integrate your phone system with other devices, such as cell phones? How can integration better serve your business? _____
_____

<table>
<tr><td>

ℛhonda's ℛule

simple is better

</td></tr>
</table>

The worksheet on page 159 will help you plan your phone needs and research special services.

Other Communication Devices

The high-tech revolution has focused on communication devices, making them smaller, less expensive, and easier to use. Some devices combine a number of services or features. Your cell phone may offer Internet access, or your handheld organizer may add phone calling capabilities. While this "convergence" of services may offer certain conveniences, be sure the quality of each service is satisfactory, the cost is competitive, and that if something goes wrong, you're not left completely isolated.

One device in particular that most businesses need and use regularly is the cell phone. Cell phones are an effective way to enable people to reach you and others — anytime. In fact, you may find that for certain employees, a cell phone is their most important phone number, and they may not need an actual phone line at all. As you plan your phone system, consider how and whether you will use cell phones as a supplement or a replacement for other phone lines.

A worksheet for comparing the costs and features of various communication devices is on page 161.

BUYING AND USING TECHNOLOGY

Technology is one part of your business you'll love and hate at the same time. Technology has enabled small companies to compete with large ones, and it has created a vast new economy of high-tech and Internet businesses. But dealing with technology can be an immense headache — decisions can be confusing and expensive to make, and difficult and expensive to change. When something goes wrong, it can affect your whole business. Good help will be hard to find.

But whether you love technology or hate it, you've got to deal with it. You don't need to become a geek or a nerd, but you've got to learn some of the basics. Just as you couldn't run a business without knowing what "accounts receivable" are, you can't run a company without being comfortable discussing Internet connections or databases.

Buying for the Long-Term

Every year I buy new equipment. And I face the same dilemma every time: with technology changing as rapidly as it does, how do I buy something that fits my budget today yet will continue to meet my needs as my business grows and changes? Should I buy an economy model, realizing I'll probably toss it aside in a year or two, or should I buy the latest, fully-loaded version?

My rule of thumb has always been to choose products I think will meet my needs and handle technology upgrades for at least two to three years. That doesn't seem like a very long time for such expensive equipment, but computers are virtually outdated the minute you get them unboxed.

How do you know what you'll need two years from now or how the technology will change in that time? It's not easy, but here are some things to ask yourself when shopping for technology:

- **What features do you absolutely have to have?** If you can't do the things you need, you've wasted money, even if you got a bargain. Consider features such as speed, size, and expandability as well as price.

- **Are your needs basic or complex?** Complicated tasks use up memory and processing speed. Word processing, running a simple bookkeeping program, and accessing e-mail and the Internet can be done on the most inexpensive computers. But creating presentations and graphics require higher-end equipment.

- **How often do you change, expand, or update software or peripherals?** You don't usually need a new computer because it's "broken," but because it can't handle the new "stuff" you want to add. If you regularly add or change

COMPARISON CHART: OTHER COMMUNICATION DEVICES

Cell phones	Provider:
Cost:	Features:
Advantages:	Disadvantages:

PDAs/Personal Organizers	Provider:
Cost:	Features:
Advantages:	Disadvantages:

Wireless Internet connections	Provider:
Cost:	Features:
Advantages:	Disadvantages:

Pagers	Provider:
Cost:	Features:
Advantages:	Disadvantages:

Radio communicators	Provider:
Cost:	Features:
Advantages:	Disadvantages:

Other	Provider:
Cost:	Features:
Advantages:	Disadvantages:

software, you want powerful hardware to handle expansion. Buy as much expansion space as you can, particularly when it comes to memory, expansion slots, and ports in the computer itself.

- **Does your new equipment have to be compatible with other equipment and software?** With stand-alone machines (such as copiers or fax machines), it may not matter if you buy an unknown brand, but with a computer or printer, you'll probably want to avoid the hassles of making an off-brand work with your other equipment.

- **Do you want single purpose or multi-function equipment?** Many pieces of equipment now handle multiple functions, such as the fax/printer/copier/scanner all-in-one. These can be a good value, especially for a younger or smaller company with limited demands.

- **Are replacement supplies readily available, and how much do they cost?** Especially with printers, fax machines and copiers, office and discount stores usually carry only the most well-known brands. Look at the cost of "consumables" such as ink and paper.

- **How cool do you want to be?** Ever since Apple introduced the iMac and made them in a variety of colors, the computer industry has started catching on to the importance of design. Consider design and ergonomics as you shop for technology.

Day-to-Day Technology Needs

Before you start shopping, you have to know what you'll be looking for. The key when selecting technology is first to outline your critical business needs and then find the solution that fits the need. Don't just get enamored of "gee whiz" technology and look for a way to use it.

Throughout this Organizer, you've outlined many of your key business functions, many of which rely on technology, such as keeping track of your finances, maintaining customer records, staying in communication. As you work through this section, focus on those tasks that can be handled or improved by technology, so that you can find the right product for that task. The worksheets on pages 164–166 will help you outline some of the technology products

you'll need for specific business functions, beginning with software.

Software and ASPs

Think through your software needs carefully. Once you've committed your business to a particular software package, it's difficult to change, either because you can't export your data easily, or because the time and effort needed to learn a new program is a barrier to making a switch.

Software. Your most basic business functions are probably best served by "off-the-shelf," widely available software programs. An accounting package, an integrated office package, and an e-mail program will get you started.

If you have specialized needs, turn to your industry association to see if there is software already developed for your type of business. Industry-specific software can be considerably more expensive than basic software, so be sure to talk with several users to find out if they're satisfied with the product.

If you have very specialized needs, you can have software designed or customized for your own use. However, customized software is more expensive to purchase and maintain, and if you have problems, you may not be able to find personnel to assist you.

ASPs. An ASP, or Application Service Provider, is essentially a software program hosted over the Internet. Instead of having the software on your own computers, you access the software (and typically the data) online. The advantage is that the software is maintained and upgraded by the provider, the initial cost may be substantially less, and you have access to your program and data wherever you have access to the Internet. The disadvantage is that you have to be online to access your program and data, it may be or feel less secure, and the overall cost in the long run may be substantially greater than if you bought a program and installed it on your own computers.

Database: One of the most important pieces of software is your database — the software that maintains your records. Of course, if you have an accounting program, this is a "database" of your finances, but you also need to look at how you'll keep track of other records — customer names and activity, inventory, suppliers, etc. You can start with something as simple as a basic mailing list package, or you may want a sophisticated customer tracking program.

Use the worksheet on pages 164–165 to identify your software/ASP needs and then to compare products as you shop for them.

Hardware

It's the rare person who gets excited about software, but it's easy to get excited about all those electronic gadgets and goodies to choose from when you look at hardware. But buying hardware can also be stressful because there are so many choices, so few sources of good information, and so much money on the line.

Once again, the thing to do is to plan before you shop. Your hardware choices should be determined by your needs and your pocketbook. I've seen new companies that start with all the latest hardware before they've even developed a product or found a customer — that's not the best way to spend money. Instead, buy what you need when you need it.

Almost every business needs the basics: computers, printers, ways to receive faxes and make copies. With multi-function machines, you may find you can use your computer and printer as a fax machine, or your fax machine as a copier. Make sure you also develop backup procedures. You may need additional hardware for that, such as disk drives.

And there's a world of "peripherals" — things such as scanners, video and digital cameras, CD recorders,

and more being invented every day. Don't feel you have to run out and buy these — a lot of us may never need them. But many of these devices can enhance your ability to do business, and indeed may be an absolute business necessity. So buy the things you really do need, even if your teenager thinks you bought it because it's "cool," and wants to borrow it.

Use the worksheet on page 166 to list your hardware needs and compare hardware equipment.

Do I Need a Network?

You may want to build your own company internal network — a local area network, or LAN — so all your computers can work together. There are many advantages to having your own network, including the ability to share office equipment, share and store data, provide security, handle Internet access, and maintain your own internal company e-mail program.

But having a network is also a bit more complicated than having stand-alone computers. You need a central computer to act as a "server," and you generally need someone who is able to maintain and support that server. You'll also need wiring to connect all the machines. Smaller and newer companies can usually get by without a network — often using the Internet itself as their network, sharing files via e-mail.

If you aren't technologically experienced, hire an experienced company or consultant to set your company network up for you — someone you can turn to on an ongoing basis for assistance. Don't depend on your brother-in-law's cousin who used to install telephones. You'll regret it.

WHAT WOULD RHONDA DO...TO ORGANIZE TECH 'STUFF'

Every time I buy a new piece of hardware or software, it comes with a host of disks, manuals, cords, installation guides, etc. Once it's out of the box, it's easy to get this stuff really confused. Before long, I don't know which extra cord goes with which machine or which disk goes with which software. So I buy extra large Ziplock™ bags and put each product's stuff in a bag of its own. With a permanent marker, I write the name of the software or hardware product and the date I purchased it on the outside of the bag. I then keep all these zipped plastic bags in one big box. I can easily find what I need if I ever have to reinstall something or refer back to the user manual.

MY SOFTWARE NEEDS			
Things to Consider:	Accounting	Contact Management	Word Processing
Which features do I need?			
Which features do I like?			
Which program offers these features at the most reasonable price?			
What is the price?			
How simple is the program to learn and operate?			
How much free technical support is available?			
How much does additional technical support cost?			
Can I find employees/consultants who know how to use it?			
Do I have enough memory (RAM and hard-drive space)?			
Does the program integrate with other hardware or software?			
How are the reviews and word-of-mouth about this program?			
Other:			

MY SOFTWARE NEEDS – CONTINUED

E-mail Program	Inventory Management	Presentation Software	Virus Protection/ Other Security

MY HARDWARE NEEDS

Use this worksheet to identify hardware you'll need in specific areas of your business. To outline your needs for communication and software products, use the worksheets on pages 161 and 164.

	General Admin./ Production	Financial/ Accounting	Sales	Other
Computers				
Printers				
Copiers/Fax Machines				
Other Peripherals (scanners, etc.)				
Internet Access Devices				
Network/ Servers				
Data storage devices				
Cables, surge protectors, back-up generators				
Other:				

WHAT WOULD RHONDA DO . . . TO GET HELP

When making a software or hardware purchase, I always look to see what kind of tech support is provided or available. Usually there's a limited amount of tech support provided for free, and an enhanced support plan for a fee. For important equipment or critical software, I always buy the additional tech support plan. That way, I have access to a knowledgeable person when something goes wrong or we have a question.

How Do I Get Help?

Without a doubt, one of the most frustrating aspects of dealing with technology is the lack of reliable, affordable, trustworthy help. Unless you have technology-proficient people on your own staff, you will be frustrated trying to find consultants or service businesses to assist you.

When selecting a consultant or technician, keep these tips in mind:

- Ask for recommendations, especially from other entrepreneurs;
- Ask how long they've been in business;
- Be cautious of those who "play around" with technology but don't do it for living;
- Be clear about how much time they have and when they'll be available to you;
- Make sure they speak in non-technical language you can understand;
- Ask them which programs and equipment they have experience with; and
- Ask if they've worked with companies in your industry before (not necessarily a requirement).

If you can find reliable consultants or technicians, use them. Especially when you are first getting started, use the assistance of a consultant to help you plan and install your equipment and software.

GETTING AND WORKING ONLINE

The Internet is part of every business in the same way as phones or the mail. It's a critical way to com-municate. The fact that the Internet can do so much more than just serve as a communication device may make it more challenging, but no business can go without using the Internet on a daily basis.

For those companies planning to conduct commerce on the Internet, I've included a separate chapter of this Organizer on e-business. This section deals with Internet questions for all companies.

Connecting

The first issue you'll face is how to connect to the Internet. The options here keep changing, so you'll want to stay abreast of your latest choices. The simplest and easiest way to get started is to use a phone "dial-up" connection, but this is not a good long-term solution for businesses that are growing, have substantial data or graphic needs, or have more than one person connected. I recommend that all but the very smallest businesses have an "always on, always fast" connection.

Regardless of the speed, or bandwidth, of your connection, you will need to deal with an Internet Service Provider (ISP). Some ISPs can host your company website, register your domain name, and provide other services, such as website design, database hosting, or writing small programs. Use the worksheet on page 168 to compare ISPs and their services.

E-mail

The number one use of the Internet is for sending and receiving e-mail. E-mail is an all-pervasive aspect of business life. Virtually all ISPs and many office-suite software programs include an e-mail program, but you do not need to use those. Recognize that you can "shop" for a different e-mail program and

COMPARISON CHART: INTERNET HOSTING COMPANIES

Use this worksheet to compare options for Internet Service Providers (ISPs).

	ISP Option #1	ISP Option #2	ISP Option #3
Company Name			
Connection Speed			
Hardware Required			
Installation Cost			
Monthly/Ongoing Fees			
Services/Capacity Provided			
Website Hosting Available			
Additional Services Available			
Reviews/ Recommendations			
Other Considerations:			

choose one that best suits your needs. Some proprietary e-mail programs, especially from free or low-cost providers, are limited in their ability to handle attachments, graphics, and large volume.

Website

The best way to build a successful website is to be clear on what you want to achieve with it — and make sure those goals are realistic. Many entrepreneurs suffer from the "if you build it, they will come syndrome," imagining that if they put up a website, they'll get a flood of new customers. That's not usually a realistic goal.

To help you understand what you can do with a site, I've classified websites into four main types:

1. **Transactional.** This is the kind of site most retailers hope for, actually selling on the net. Perhaps the best known example is bookseller Amazon.com. The problem with trying to get customers to buy on your site is that running an online store is just like running a "land-based" store: it's usually a full-time job, and you have to spend time and money getting people to your location. You also have to learn how to display and sell your merchandise on a site, just like in a real store. For more on running a "transactional" website, go to the e-business chapter of this Organizer.

2. **Promotional.** Perhaps you're dreaming your website can attract new customers from all over the world who'll find you while surfing the net. This happens in certain industries, such as travel, where customers are willing to spend a long time sifting through sites to do research. I found and booked a London hotel on the Internet, but it took an entire evening. Promotional sites also work for "niche" businesses that offer a relatively hard-to-find item or service. If you're hoping to find new customers with a promotional site, ask yourself: "Will people really spend a long time to find a business like mine?"

3. **Informational.** One of the best uses of a website is to give information about your company to potential customers and employees who hear about you "offline." I found a graphic designer by asking friends for recommendations, and then checking websites. After visiting www.longdesign.com, I chose Jennifer Long. Jennifer's site serves as a combination brochure and portfolio, including references from past clients. I didn't even interview anyone without a website. Your website can be extensive and detailed, or just include the basic information, but an informational website enables customers to find out about you, and it gives you a measure of credibility.

4. **Relational.** Finally, a website can be a good way to build closer relationships with current customers. You can post specials, provide detailed information on topics relating to your services, and put up a FAQ list (frequently asked questions). If you have more technical capabilities, you can add forms so customers can communicate with you, track orders, or see work-in-progress.

When planning your website, keep in mind not only the initial design and cost of the site, but the ongoing maintenance. Don't design a site that requires continual changes or updates unless you have the staff and resources to handle that. Remember, most companies can succeed very well with a simple website that describes the company's services and products, basic details, and answers to most-asked questions.

Use the worksheet on page 170 to plan the functions and information you want on your website.

WORKING AT A DISTANCE

A few years ago, I realized that in my consulting practice, I had clients all over the U.S. and even internationally, but for an entire year, I didn't have one client in my home state of California. Today, I have employees in several different states.

Doing business long distance is a critical skill, even for the smallest of enterprises. Clients are more comfortable working with distant companies, employees can be located in other states, and with a website, you have no geographic boundaries. With a little planning, you can run an international operation, even from a home office. Here are the essentials:

MY WEBSITE CHECKLIST

Use this worksheet to describe what things you want to include on your website.

✔	Website Information/Features	Details/Description
	Company Description	
	Products/Services Description	
	Product Pictures	
	Pricing	
	Contact Info, Address and Phone Number	
	Map to location	
	Portfolio/Work Samples	
	Client List	
	Press clips	
	FAQ (frequently asked questions)	
	Key employee bios	
	Job opportunities	
	Reliability/Trust seals	
	Customer bulletin boards	
	Password protected client areas	
	Password protected employee areas	
	Site map	
	Investor relations	
	Other:	

- **E-mail.** The Internet has made it easy to stay in touch and also to send and receive documents, graphics, even presentations instantly and free. Problems arise if you and your distant correspondent don't have compatible software or don't share files in compatible formats. Try sending and opening attachments in different formats long before you're on deadline.

- **Document sharing.** If you have a website, you can upload documents, presentations, graphics, etc., to show or share them with others at a distance. You can also create password protected sections of your website to share certain items only with selected others, such as individual clients.

- **Overnight services.** One of the key contributors to the growth of small and home-based businesses has been the introduction of overnight delivery services, such as FedEx. If you work with distant employees or customers, you'll be a regular user of these services.

- **Time differences.** One of the most difficult aspects of working long distance is juggling time zones. You'll have to make some accommodation — working later on the East Coast, earlier on the West. Here's an important trick: whenever you leave messages for those you don't work with regularly, indicate which time zone you're in.

- **Phones.** It's virtually impossible to do business long distance without using the phone. Even if you're a power e-mail user, actually talking to someone builds relationships and prevents misunderstandings, so don't hesitate to pick up that phone!

- **Face Time.** Airplanes are still full in this Internet age because nothing beats getting to know someone face-to-face. If you can, always meet your major customers and suppliers in person. For ongoing relationships, especially with remotely-located employees or subcontractors, set up regular travel times to work together.

Working long distance is easier and much cheaper than it used to be, which in turn influences your decisions about where to locate and who to hire. That flexibility can also give your business a tremendous competitive edge.

Summary

The world really has become a much smaller place for business, and that makes communication even more important. Whether you're working with an employee across the room or a customer around the globe, develop ways to stay in touch on a regular basis. Communication provides reassurance, motivation, support, and acknowledgement.

Most communication will use some form of technology. And all kinds of technology are important in business today. While choices in technology may seem confusing and ever-changing, it's all those electronic devices and software that has made much of the growth of entrepreneurship possible. One key component of your technology planning is your website and use of the Internet.

So get connected!

MY WILD IDEAS

Wild Ideas about Communications:

Wild Ideas about Technology:

good company

Every entrepreneur wants to build a good company, one that produces a great product or service, makes money, and earns market share. But running a good company also involves a level of responsibility — to your customers, employees, and the community at large. When your company does good — treats people fairly, participates in community and charitable activities, and adheres to ethical business practices — it can become a great company.

Businesses that act with integrity and honesty are more likely to have their employees act with integrity and honesty towards the company and their fellow workers. Your company is less likely to get in trouble with regulatory agencies or taxing authorities or to face law suits or fines.

And employees themselves value being part of an organization that is committed to enhancing the social good. Prospective employees look at a company's values and social commitment when comparing job offers, and you enhance the long-term value of your company when you can attract and retain the employees you want.

Corporate social responsibility is:

- Good for business
- Good for the community
- Good for the economy

Being socially responsible is part of the overall health of your company, and it is the right thing to do. There's always strength in doing the right thing.

HOW CAN I BE A GOOD CORPORATE CITIZEN?

Corporations are unique entities with many rights and privileges. Society, through its laws, grants corporations special and favorable benefits, such as the limits on personal liability of a corporation's shareholders. Society, in the form of consumers, patronizes businesses, giving them market share and profits. Every business, then, relies on the continuing support of society for its growth and success.

Good corporate citizenship begins with a company's own internal practices and policies. It starts with corporate integrity. Key areas of business in which you can focus your efforts include:

- **Employees.** Treat employees fairly and with respect; compensate employees fairly; consider the well-being of employees as part of your decision-making;
- **Customers.** Be honest and fair to your customers and suppliers, and in your advertising and marketing;

RED TAPE ALERT!

Discrimination. It's not good business. It's not good behavior. And it's against the law. In virtually all situations, it is illegal to discriminate against employees because of race, religion, sex, or national origin. In many situations, it's illegal to discriminate on the basis of age, physical disability, or sexual orientation. You may not discriminate in hiring, promotion, pay, or treatment. Moreover, it is your responsibility as an employer to create an environment that is not hostile to any individual or group based on such factors. You must also make "reasonable accommodation" to employees' religious observance needs, such as allowing them time off on their sabbaths or holy days or wearing articles of religious attire (unless there is a significant safety concern). Ask your attorney about conforming to regulations laid out in the Civil Rights Act, Americans with Disabilities Act (ADA), and other anti-discrimination laws.

- **Community.** Be involved in your community and concerned about the well-being of others; and
- **Environment.** Be cognizant of the impact your actions have on the environment.

Develop an Ethics Policy

Most companies, especially large corporations now develop clear ethics guidelines and policies. Because employees are faced with many situations that have ethical implications, it is extremely useful to have a set of clear consistent policies that are firmly and fairly enforced throughout the company.

For a new or small company, an ethics policy doesn't have to be complex, but when you establish clear guidelines on issues such as respecting customer confidentiality or receiving gifts, gratuities, or special favors, you help avoid conflict or legal trouble.

If you are doing business internationally, you will also face issues of local laws or culture. How do you expect your employees to behave in those situations?

New technological developments present new ethical challenges. It's much easier to accumulate, buy, or share data on customers. Technology also makes it simple, cheap, even inviting to copy others' copyrighted works, such as software, music, data, or written work. The laws on some copyright issues are in flux, so you may not be certain if copying a certain item is legal. See the section on intellectual property on page 145, and check with your attorney if you are unsure about issues relating to copyright.

The worksheet on page 175 helps you articulate the key issues of your Ethics Policy.

DEALING WITH CUSTOMERS

The basic obligation you have to your customers is to provide them with quality goods and services — to deliver what you sell. It's your responsibility to make sure you're not selling shoddy or unsafe products or services.

To reassure customers they can depend on your company, you may want to offer guarantees or warranties of your products or services. Of course, you must then honor those guarantees. But even more important than offering a guarantee is first taking all necessary steps to ensure the quality of your products or services.

Some of these steps include:

- Designing your products or services to achieve the results desired and advertised;

Rhonda's Rule
it's easier to avoid getting into trouble than to get out of it

MY ETHICS POLICY

Describe how you will ensure your company and employees obey the law and behave ethically in the following areas:

Legal Dealings: How will you ensure that your company obeys the laws not only of your home country but also of other countries in which your company does business?

Employees: How will you ensure that you and your managers treat employees fairly, honestly, and with respect? How will you ensure that subcontractors act ethically? What guidelines will you establish for the personal use of company property, such as company cars, phones, or e-mail?

Customers: What actions will you take to deal honestly with customers? How will ensure truth in advertising? How will you instruct employees to deal with gifts, special favors, meals, etc. from customers or vendors?

Community: How will your company take into account the impact of its actions on the community?

Environment: How will your company take into account the impact of its actions on the environment, including in its choice of suppliers, manufacturing, distribution, and waste disposal?

- Ensuring high and consistent quality of manufacture and production so that the design specifications can be met;

- Using reliable and trustworthy suppliers and subcontractors so that the materials and outsourced production are of sufficient quality;

- Taking steps to continually improve quality and respond to any problems, defects, or complaints.

Advertising and Sales Practices

Your responsibility to your customers begins even before they buy from you — with what you tell them about your products, services, or your company itself. Many companies get in trouble because they use misleading, confusing, or even false advertising or sales techniques to attract customers. This is bad business, often illegal, and a sure formula for complaints.

Sometimes you may not be intentionally dishonest, just eager to make a sale. You or your company may overstate or overpromise what you can deliver. You may believe so strongly in your product or service that you unfairly and inaccurately compare yourself to the competition.

Before you begin an advertising program, and as you train your sales personnel, familiarize yourself with what constitutes deceptive or dishonest marketing. The Better Business Bureau has worked with the advertising industry as well as leading corporations to develop an advertising code, which you can find at www.bbb.org/advertising/adcode.asp.

Customer Complaints

Of course, we'd like every client or customer to be fully satisfied with our products or services, and be eager to do business with us again. But the reality is, sooner or later, we're going to have some unhappy customers.

It's tempting to dismiss dissatisfied customers as chronic complainers. "I'm better off without their business," you may think. Instead, view customer complaints as opportunities to improve. If a customer never tells you of a problem, you can't correct it. Customer complaints can be a valuable resource for improving your company's performance

Most unhappy customers don't complain — they just take their business elsewhere. But don't assume they leave quietly. Studies show a dissatisfied customer will tell an average of 8–16 others about their negative experience. As if that's not bad enough, a report of a bad experience is twice as likely to affect someone's buying decision as a good report. So every unhappy customer is a walking marketing machine — for your competitors.

By developing a customer feedback and complaint handling procedure you can turn negative situations into opportunities to build customers for life. In your complaint program, incorporate some or all of the following principles:

- **Apologize.** Saying "We're sorry" is an important first step in letting customers know you care when they have a problem.

- **Don't blame the customer.** "You ordered the wrong thing." "You didn't follow directions." Even if the customer isn't always right, they always believe they are. Most misunderstandings are due to poor explanations on the part of your salespeople. When you blame a customer, they see it as a personal attack.

- **Admit your errors and solve the problem.** Every business makes mistakes; you will too. Just be determined to get to the root of the problem and make it better for the customer. If something is wrong, fix it.

- **Don't use the excuse, "It's company policy."** No phrase is more dismissive to customers than to be told they won't be treated as individuals. The only policy your company should have when dealing with complaints is, "We do our very best to solve every problem."

- **Give front-line sales and service people authority.** My friend returned an $8 bath rug to a department store and had to go to three offices to get her money back. The store was trying to protect against employee theft, but their bureaucratic policies lost a customer forever. Empower employees to solve minor problems.

BETTER BUSINESS BUREAU CHECKLIST

Use this checklist to gauge how prepared your company is to handle complaints and resolve disputes. Have a strategy in place to deal with complaints and resolve disputes quickly.

	Are complaint handling procedures clearly understood by all employees?
	Has a person been designated to supervise complaint handling activity?
	Are there clear, written procedures for screening and logging, investigating, acknowledging, resolving, responding to, and following-up complaints?
	Is there a known procedure for referring unsettled complaints to a third party dispute resolution mechanism?
	Do the procedures cover complaints by mail, by phone, online, or in person?
	Have you considered installing an 800 telephone number or online complaint form to aid in customer service and complaint handling?
	Are there management controls to ensure that complaints are processed according to policy and procedures?
	Do the controls ensure prompt handling and settlement of complaints within a reasonable time frame?
	Are communications to customers handled in a helpful and courteous manner and can you ensure prompt and complete answers to customer questions?
	Has there been any analysis by management of past complaints to identify patterns, trends, and causes?
	Does the manner of complaint handling represent the best interests of the company, as well as its customers?

Copyright © 2000, Council of Better Business Bureaus. Reprinted with permission.

- **Encourage feedback.** Make it easy for customers to let you know how they feel. Many companies now give customers cards to rate the service and make comments. This also gives customers an opportunity to let you know what you're doing right.

- **Don't be cheap.** Correcting mistakes is a normal and necessary cost of doing business. Trying to save a few dollars but losing a customer is penny wise and pound foolish. While there may be a small percentage of customers who will take advantage of you, the majority will be even more loyal if they know you'll fix problems when they arise.

Dispute Resolution

A significant conflict with a customer, employee, supplier, or partner is always disrupting, and the more we allow disagreements to escalate, the more damaging they become. When the conflict becomes too drawn out, expensive, or bitter, even the eventual "victor" may feel like they've lost. So here's my advice when involved in conflict:

- **Remember Rhonda's Rule: "Settle for Victory."** By this I mean concentrate on finding a positive outcome for yourself and settle for that. It's easy to become obsessed with "winning" — defeating the other guy, proving them wrong, making them pay. But those things may not be necessary for a positive outcome for you. Stay

Rhonda's Rule

settle for victory

WHAT WOULD RHONDA DO. . . TO RESOLVE DISPUTES

I've been in business disputes, and I can tell you it's not fun. Even little disputes can cause you to lose sleep. Big ones cause you to lose money, business, even friends. The best thing is to try hard to avoid disputes in the first place. Before entering into a relationship (customer, partner, employee, strategic alliance) clarify all the terms, being certain to discuss areas of potential conflict. Then put it in writing! If a dispute arises, sit down and see if you can work things out. If you can, once again put it in writing then and there. If not, find a neutral or friendly person to act as a neutral party to help you work things out. AVOID LAWSUITS! Even if you're totally in the right, you can lose a bundle — even your business — proving it. Use "Alternative Dispute Resolution" — mediation or arbitration. Check out the Better Business Bureau's "BBB DR" service in your area. BBBs offer low-cost or free dispute resolution services for their members.

focused on your long-term best interests. If you'd rather be right than rich, you probably will be.

- **Don't take things personally.** Even the most reasonable, fair, easy-going people find themselves the target of complaints. It happens. I know it's tough not to take it as a personal attack, but try to focus on the issues not the personalities — even if the other guy's a jerk.

- **Look for the quickest solution first.** Even if it seems more expensive at first, the quickest resolution is frequently the best. The longer you're involved in a dispute, the more costly and more disruptive to your business and your life it becomes. You need to be building and running your business, not fighting.

- **Avoid lawsuits.** Even if you have the law firmly and completely on your side, lawsuits are expensive and debilitating. While it may be a good idea to get legal advice and consult a lawyer, be very slow to actually file a lawsuit or even threaten one. Try to keep disputes from escalating to the point that your adversary wants to initiate legal action. Try not to make a federal case out of it.

- **Explore alternative dispute resolution mechanisms.** If things really get out of hand, instead of going to court, try mediation or arbitration. These are less expensive and often less poisonous to ongoing relationships. Mediation provides for a neutral party to assist you in discussing resolutions, but the result is not binding. Arbitra-

tion typically means both sides abide by the decision of the arbitrator.

COMMUNITY INVOLVEMENT

Many companies, including new entrepreneurial ventures, are developing creative ways to act on their social commitment and contribute to their community. For example, the Internet company eBay, before their IPO (Initial Public Offering) of stock to the public, set aside a fair amount of company stock to establish a philanthropic foundation. As eBay's stock rose dramatically, the value of their foundation also rose.

You have many options for choosing how your company can get involved in community or charitable activities. Be sure to involve employees themselves in choosing the projects and policies. Discuss how your company's values intersect with your programs.

While your company is young and/or small, you may want to limit your social activities to simple things: after all, you do have a company to build. You might only select one-time activities that could involve all members of your company as a team, such as participating in a walk for a community charity or volunteering one day to work on building a house for Habitat for Humanity. These can help

MY PLAN FOR COMMUNITY INVOLVEMENT

Use this worksheet to develop a plan for community involvement that coincides with your personal and business goals and values.

✔	**What are your business goals?**	**Description/Details**
	Visibility in community	
	Visibility in industry	
	Enhancing employee morale/employee involvement	
	Developing contacts with other companies	
	Aid in recruiting employees	
	Other:	

✔	**In what ways will you participate?**	**Description/Details**
	Donate money from operating budget	
	Donate a set percentage of profits/sales, in-kind products or services, or company facilities for use by community groups	
	Participate as a company in community events	
	Allow employees to be active in projects on paid time	
	Formulate socially responsible operations (e.g. waste disposal management) or purchasing practices (e.g., environmental-friendly only products or type of vendor)	
	Encourage employees to be active on a volunteer basis/after-hours	
	Encourage company personnel/management to serve on agency boards	
	Other:	

✔	**What types of concerns do you want to be involved with?**				
	Animal Welfare		Environment		Economic Empowerment
	The Arts		Gender Equality/Issues		Education
	Children		Health Issues		Safety
	Community Improvement		Recreation/Athletics		Other:

promote team spirit, but the time commitment is clear and limited.

You can also choose an ongoing project that is not too demanding; one new company gives an hour a week to help out at a local school. As your company grows, you may choose more ambitious projects.

Some companies find being socially responsible is a critical component of their business concept. They develop a strategic position in the marketplace based on their actions or policies, such as developing organic baby food, non-animal-tested cosmetics, or non-polluting electric cars. Other companies plan key marketing campaigns around social issues, such as an Internet company drawing traffic to their site by giving an amount for each visitor to support a certain social cause.

RESPECT FOR THE ENVIRONMENT

An important part of being a good corporate citizen is respecting the world we all live in. Businesses are discovering that being environmentally friendly is not only good for the world; it's good for the bottom line. It saves money and boosts employee morale.

Developing environmentally-friendly policies is often more a matter of attitude and awareness than having to make major changes. Sometimes even simple solutions can make a significant difference. For example, you can:

- **Reduce waste and pollution.** Although you may not think of them this way, waste and pollution actually represent something you bought, couldn't or didn't sell, and now have to get rid of. You've been paying for resources you haven't fully consumed (or the customer won't consume), whether it's manufacturing waste, excess packaging, or just a lot of trash. The simplest, most cost efficient, and environmentally-sound step is to reduce waste. Look around — what do you "waste" that could be used? One example of a

small company that rooted out waste was the Crib Diaper Service in Crystal, Minnesota. Like any diaper service, they generated tons of lint from washing and drying all those diapers. They used to throw the lint away, but lint is just cotton, and the employees were frustrated by the waste. They came up with a novel solution: the company sells the lint to a local casket company that uses it to make cotton batting for coffin lining. True womb to tomb recycling!

- **Lower energy use.** Unnecessary or excessive energy use is another form of waste. If you can produce your products or services or run your operation with less energy consumption, then you've saved money at the same time you're helping the environment.

- **Encourage employees to walk, bike, or use public transportation.** The biggest impact you may have on the environment happens before anyone even arrives at the office: driving to work. Find ways for employees to use alternative modes of transportation, and consider access to public transportation when you choose a location.

- **Buy environmentally-friendly supplies and materials.** One of the simplest things you can do to help the environment is to purchase environmentally-friendly supplies — whether that means using recycled paper or finding environmentally-friendly sources of raw materials for your manufacturing process. Look for products that don't use animal testing. Get toner cartridges for printers and copiers refilled instead of throwing them out, and recycle old computers by donating them to local schools or nonprofit organizations.

Summary

You can help your company do well by doing good. Companies gain respect, enhance customer loyalty, and increase employee morale by engaging in responsible business practices: acting honestly, treating customers fairly, and being involved in their community and world. It also helps keep you out of trouble. Being a good company is good business.

MY WASTE REDUCTION AND ENVIRONMENTAL POLICY

Describe your policies in each of the following areas

Energy Use
Water Use
Recycling
Waste Disposal
Waste Reduction
Purchasing Policies
Commute/Transportation/Parking Issues
Ensuring subcontractors/Independent Contractors follow similar policies?
Other:

MY WILD IDEAS FOR BEING A GOOD COMPANY

home office

For 14 years, I ran my business — or should I say businesses — from home. I started a consulting practice, built and sold one Internet company, and founded a publishing company. But I never had more than what I jokingly called my "one room commute."

When I finally decided to lease office space, I left home with some regret. Running a business from home has its challenges, but it has its pleasures as well. You get the advantage of a truly integrated life, save time commuting, and get more flexibility in dealing with family obligations.

The key is to set up a home office right. In my 14 years working from home, I learned many tricks on how to run a great home office. If you are preparing to set up a home office, this chapter discusses some of the issues you'll face.

If you spend much of your workday on the road, and your vehicle — a car, truck, or van — serves as your office (or one of your offices), this chapter discusses some of your issues as well.

Rhonda's Rule

know when to leave the "office" — even when you work from home

---

HOW DO I FIND THE SPACE TO WORK?

A home office can take many forms. It might simply be one end of your dining room table. It could be the guest room, as long as no guests come to visit! You might claim a section of your garage, and even build in walls and install a window, shelves, heating, and air conditioning.

If you're serious about your business, you need good work space. You don't necessarily need a separate room, but find a space without too many distractions.

Once you've chosen the physical space for your office, consider what will go in it:

- **A desk or work table.** At the very minimum, you should have a desk or table used only for work. Having to clear your stuff off the dining room table every night quickly gets old. Make certain it's the right height for what you're doing.

- **A good chair.** Get out of that folding chair and buy yourself something comfortable enough to sit in for hours.

- **Good lighting.** Most homes don't have sufficient lighting to work and read all day, so in addition to overhead and indirect lighting, get a task

RED TAPE ALERT!

If you are producing products at your home office, you face a set of issues you should discuss with a lawyer: zoning, shipping, and environmental regulations. Be careful! Obviously, if yours is a small crafts business,much like a hobby craft, no one is going to notice or particularly care. But if you are making anything that can be noticed by others, you may incur the wrath of neighbors and the attention of city authorities. Even things you engaged in as a hobby before — fixing cars, carpentry, etc. — can offend neighbors when they know you're now doing this as business. Remember Rhonda's Rule: get to know a lawyer.

light for your desk. Don't put your computer monitor directly in front of a window (you'll squint all day), and watch for glare from other windows.

- **Heaters or air conditioners.** The temperature in your office is more than just a matter of personal comfort (which is very important). If you have equipment in your office, you need a stable and moderate temperature. I crashed a hard drive because my office was in a room that got very cold at night and condensation formed on the drive.

- **Storage.** When you run a business from home, you accumulate stuff — a lot of stuff! You need someplace to put it. Buy an office-type storage cabinet or put shelves up in a closet. Put stuff you need frequently within easy reach. Trust me, you'll underestimate the amount of storage space you need.

- **Electricity.** Surge protector strips have the benefit of increasing the number of your electrical outlets, but be careful not to overload circuits. Buy the kind of surge protectors that can handle 'transformers' — those big electrical plugs on many technology devices.

- **Wiring.** If you're going to use a high-speed Internet connection, have more than one person connected at a time, or use your connection in more than one room, you may want to wire your space for ethernet connections. If you're remodeling or moving into new space, discuss wiring first!

This list doesn't even begin to address two other vital components of a home office: your phone and computer systems. Many of those concerns are discussed

in the chapter on Technology and Communications, but a home office does present some unique issues.

HOW MANY PHONE LINES DO I NEED?

Of course, whether you need to get a second phone line is just the tip of the iceberg regarding your home office telecommunications needs. But this is the question many people ask as they wire their home office for a fax machine, voice mail, and Internet connection. In fact, many entrepreneurs already have a second phone line and are asking themselves if they should get a third!

Once your toddler answers a call from your most important client, you'll see the necessity of a separate line for incoming business calls. And if you want to be listed in the *Yellow Pages* or "business" section of the phone book, most local phone companies require you to have a "business" line. If you receive a lot of faxes or use a dial-up modem, get a separate data line as well.

Above all, if being on the Internet is at all important to your business, get a fast Internet connection. Look into whether an internet service provider (ISP) in your area offers DSL or cable modem service. This enables you to be on the Internet continually without tying up a phone line.

In a home office, you also face the issue of what kind of voice mail to have and what the message should say. An extra phone line for business enables you to have

MY HOME OFFICE SPACE PLAN

Where will I locate my desk/workspace?

Where will I store my daily work materials?

Where will I place my computer?

My monitor?

My printer?

My fax?

My copier?

✔	Issue	My Solution
	Climate Control	
	Lighting/Glare	
	Meeting Clients	
	Phone Wiring	
	Internet Wiring	
	Electrical Wiring	
	Storage Space	
	Other:	

HOME OFFICE SHOPPING LIST

✔	Item	Details
	Desks/worktables	
	Chairs	
	Computer	
	Monitor	
	Phones	
	Printer	
	Copier	
	Fax	
	Scanner	
	Storage cabinet	
	Storage bins	
	File cabinets	
	Bookshelves	
	Task Light	
	Overhead lights	
	Glare screen	
	Cables/extension cords, etc.	
	Answering Machine/Voice Mail	
	Office supplies:	
	Pens/Pencils	
	Paper	
	Toner Cartridges	
	Calculator	
	Blank disks, CDs, etc.	
	Other:	
	Other:	
	Other:	
	Other:	

WHAT WOULD RHONDA DO . . . TO SET UP PHONE LINES

If you live with any other people, you'll probably need a second — or third — phone line. I like having three phone lines: one for business, one for personal, and one for data/fax. Once I got a high-speed Internet connection, the third line was less critical. Having a business line allowed me to be listed in the business section and Yellow Pages, but since the phone company charges a lot more for calls on a business line, I made my outgoing calls on the personal line and used the "business" line for incoming calls. I prefer voice mail over answering machines because they are more reliable in case of a power or phone line outage. And buy a good, multi-line phone from an office supply store, one where you can put callers on hold and conduct conference calls.

a business message on that line and a family message on your other line. If you have to share one incoming line for both business and family, carefully consider whether you really want your clients and colleagues to hear a message recorded by your three-year-old.

HOW DO I MEET WITH CUSTOMERS?

If you work out of your home, one of the biggest challenges is often figuring out where and when to meet with customers. If you only meet customers at their place of business, at trade shows, or over the Internet, no problem! But if customers are going to come to you, how will you arrange your space so you look professional?

If you're going to be meeting with others regularly, ideally, you want to set up your work space separately from your family surroundings. If possible, have a separate entrance or at least a path to your office that doesn't go through a messy playroom. If you're meeting clients infrequently, or on a regular schedule, you may be able to use your own living or dining room as a meeting space. Just make sure the rest of the family, if any, know to stay away!

What if you don't want customers in your home but need to meet them somewhere other than their offices? Look for other, "neutral" locations, such as meeting them over lunch in a restaurant. If you have an ongoing need, find another company that will

allow you to "sublet" or "rent" a meeting space or conference room on an hourly basis (such as a small law firm). "Executive suite" services — short-term office rentals — often offer hourly rentals as well.

SHOULD I GET A BUSINESS MAIL BOX?

When I first started working from home, I wasn't comfortable giving my address to strangers I met at networking gatherings or putting it on a marketing brochure. At that time, the only alternative I knew was to rent a post office box from the U.S. Postal Service.

I was afraid, however, that having my only address be a "P.O. Box" would look like I wasn't a serious business. In addition, the Post Office usually doesn't accept mail from private delivery services such as Federal Express or UPS. I felt I had no choice, so I used my home address. That was 1986. Since 1990, I've had a better solution. I rent a mailbox from a private mailbox company (also called a "commercial mail receiving agency" or CMRA) such as Mailboxes, Etc.

A private mailbox gives you the advantage of not giving out your home address, having a secure place to receive mail, and having someone there who can sign for and receive packages for you. They often offer other services for additional fees, such as forwarding mail, calling you if you receive a special delivery, and allowing you to call in and check your mail if you're on the road.

OFFICE IN A TRUCK, VAN, OR CAR

What will I be using my mobile office to do: (check those that apply)

	Make Phone calls		Write up orders		Use computer
	Open mail		Carry passengers		Store samples/
	Store supplies		Haul equipment		Other hauling
	Other Issues:				

Other issues: (check those that apply)

✔	Issue	My Solution:
	Cell Phone	
	Storage	
	Writing surface	
	Office supplies	
	Climate control	
	Security	
	Safety	
	Insurance	
	Computer use	
	Internet connection	
	Parking	
	Other issues:	

One other advantage: with a private mailbox, you can usually use their address, followed by the symbol "#" or the word number and your box number, so that you don't have to use the term "P.O. Box" as your address. (For example, my post box address is 555 Bryant St, #180, Palo Alto, CA 94301). Just be sure to verify with your mailbox service before you print business cards as to what is allowed.

WORKING FROM THE ROAD

Many businesses are actually run not from an office or from home but from a car, van, or truck. In some industries and lines of work — contractors, sales representatives, real estate agents, landscape designers, to name a few — an efficient and workable mobile office is a necessity.

But since many people do not think of their car, van, or truck as their "office," they don't plan for it, and quickly find their workplace unworkable, with important notes shoved in the glove compartment or valuable equipment moving around loose in the back of their truck.

So if you know you're going to be using your vehicle for business, develop a mobile office plan, using the worksheet on page 188 to assist you. Figure out your needs first and then look for solutions that are affordable and will work for you. Because so many people work from mobile offices, there are many commercially available products to outfit cars and trucks for specific purposes, including most kinds of contractors or trades. There are even "desks" for your front seat.

Since your vehicle is your office, you'll also want to assure its contents are safe. You probably don't want to store the only copy of valuable documents or records in your vehicle. Consider where you will park and store your vehicle, and make certain your insurance covers not only the vehicle itself but also your "office" contents or equipment. And, of course, ask your tax advisor about deductions for your mobile office.

WHAT TAX DEDUCTIONS CAN I TAKE?

When you work from home, one murky area you'll quickly deal with is which expenses are deductible as business expenses and which aren't. If you buy a new work table that you use for both your office and for the kids' homework projects, is that deductible? If you add a space heater to your office in the garage, can you deduct the extra utility expenses? What if you let your kids use your office supplies?

Tax deductions for home offices are daunting and confusing. As always, I strongly suggest you discuss all the tax issues with an accountant before you even begin your business, make any changes to your home, or buy any furniture or equipment. As mentioned in the "Getting Started" chapter of this book, start-up expenses for a business must be "capitalized," or spread out over the first five years of your business. This is also true for setting up your home office. So you may want to get your business underway before spending a great deal of money.

Most normal business expenses that you would incur whether or not you were working from home — postage, office supplies, advertising, wages — are treated the same way as any other business. You can deduct those expenses as part of your regular deductions for the cost of doing business.

However, you have an additional tax savings option on your home office if you qualify — the home office deduction. But since there are so many other considerations with the home office deduction, including the fact that it's rigorously examined by taxing authorities, and you may face tax implications if you later sell your home, you certainly want to discuss whether you should take or skip the deduction with your tax advisor.

Take the Test

There are two conditions under which you can take a tax deduction for business use of part of your home: exclusive use and non-exclusive use.

Answer the following questions as part of the exclusive use test:

❏ You use part of your residence regularly and exclusively for business purposes

Plus, at least one of the following apply:

❏ You use a portion of your home as your principal place of business (including administrative or managerial activities that are not conducted at any other location).

❏ You use your home as a place to meet clients, customers, or patients.

❏ Your home office is a separate structure that is not attached to your house or living quarters.

Two non-exclusive uses also qualify you to take some tax deduction for business use of your home:

❏ Storage of inventory — a wholesaler or retailer who uses part of a home to store inventory if the dwelling unit is the taxpayer's sole fixed location of the trade or business; or

❏ Day care facility — part of the home is used for day care of children, physically and mentally disabled persons, or individuals age 65 or older.

For these and other tax issues, talk to your accountant. Use the guide "Questions to Ask…On Home Office Deductions" to get your conversation started.

HOW DO I SEPARATE WORK AND HOME LIFE?

One of the most difficult tasks for people who work from home is establishing a clear distinction between work and home. If you're not disciplined, you may find yourself distracted by non-business matters. One friend said her house was never cleaner than when she worked from home; she did housework to avoid doing business.

On the other hand, many people who work from home find they never leave "work." They end up working day and night, much to the annoyance of family and friends.

Separating your work and home life can be especially difficult when you live with others: a spouse, children, or guests who come to visit. Friends and relatives often view home-workers as always available, and don't understand why, in the middle of a work day, you can't run an errand for them, go to a movie, or pick up their kids from school.

The best way to deal with working at home is to try to be as professional as possible while still allowing yourself some of the freedom and flexibility you want to achieve.

QUESTIONS TO ASK . . . ON HOME OFFICE DEDUCTIONS

- What percentage of my rent or mortgage can I deduct?
- Can I deduct costs of remodeling? Rewiring?
- Can I deduct these expenses the first year, or do I have to capitalize them over a number of years?
- Is it wise for me to take the home office deduction?
- What are the tax implications if I later sell my home?
- What percentage of my phone or Internet connection costs can I deduct?
- What percentage of my utilities or other expenses can I deduct?
- What furniture and equipment expenses are deductible? Office supplies?
- What transportation expenses can I deduct for getting from my office to customers?
- Can I deduct expenses for artwork, décor, stereos, or other amenities in my home office?
- What other business expenses can I deduct?

MY HOME OFFICE POLICIES

Work hours when I can't be interrupted:

Work hours when I can be interrupted:

Hours when I definitely will NOT work:

Which phone lines can NOT be answered by any others?

Which phone lines CAN be answered by others? When?

What should someone say to they answer the phone? (example: "John Smith's office, Larry speaking," or "555-1313, May I help you?")

What is the message on your voice mail/answering machine? (is it a family or a business message?)

What hours will I NOT answer my work line?

What area is to be used ONLY for my work?

When are others allowed to use my work area?

What other areas will I use? What times? When will I NOT use other areas?

How many days/weeks a year will I take off for vacation?

When is my busiest time of day/week/year? How will those change work/family interaction?

When can I be responsible for child care? When can I not?

What constitutes an "emergency"?

Other:

Establish Work Hours

The most important step to protect your valuable personal time and work time is to set work hours. Make sure that you, your clients, employees, friends, and family know what your work hours are, when and why you can be interrupted, when you'll take days off, and when your busiest time of the day, week, or year is (so they can leave you alone!).

Structure your day and week. Set a work routine that makes you, your family, and others more aware that you're really working: "I start work right after I take the kids to school; take a break around 10:30; lunch around 1 PM, go to the post office and run errands from 4 to 6 PM and catch up on paperwork at 9 PM. On Tuesdays and Thursdays, I leave work early to go to exercise class."

Be Clear with Guests about Your Spare Time

Whether your office is in the guest room or the next town, having guests can be a strain on the entrepreneur. Often, guests don't understand how self-employed people structure their workdays or work weeks.

Allow yourself some fun time to spend with your visitors, but be clear with your guests about when you'll be with them and the limits on your availability. Let prospective guests know ahead of time how much time you'll be able to spend with them, so they'll understand the situation before they arrive. Put this in the most positive light: "I'm delighted I've been able to cancel my meetings for Thursday afternoon to spend with you. Until then, I'm sure you'll enjoy exploring the city on your own." If you need, make up a list of sights or keep brochures on hand so visitors can find ways to entertain themselves.

KIDS AND THE HOME OFFICE

Many parents find the greatest appeal of a home office is being home for the kids. However, I have also heard many former work-from-home parents tell me how, after a year or so of working from home, an office away from home became a vital expense.

Noise Control

Often, the most irritating, and potentially costly, aspect of having kids invade your work space at home is the noise they create. If you are talking on the phone to a client, investor, or employee, you need to maintain professionalism, and you don't want them to hear kids screaming in the background.

If you are making or expecting an important phone call, keep kids out of ear-shot. If an important phone call comes in unexpectedly, put the caller on hold until you get to a quiet room.

Make Child Care Arrangements

Be realistic about the demands that both kids and your business place on you. Don't expect to get work done with kids coming in and out, wanting to be driven places, needing a snack, or wanting you to help them settle an argument. Don't imagine, either, that you can hand your kids off to a neighbor; if you do, tomorrow the neighbors' kids will be in your backyard.

Some types of work have more flexibility in terms of deadlines, work hours, or customer phone calls. Others are truly difficult to manage when you have a demanding two-year-old or teenager.

As a work-at-home parent, you have some added flexibility in child care arrangements that typical office workers don't have. If you have school-aged children, you may be able to schedule your work hours from 9:00 AM – 3:00 PM, then spend time with the kids, and return to work at 8:00 PM, when they've gone to bed. You may be able to share child care responsibilities with a spouse — caring for them during the day, and retreating to your home office at 5:00 PM when your spouse gets home from work.

Whatever your arrangement, develop a structured routine for your kids that keeps them busy (and out of your hair) for a set period of time each week so you can get work done. Since it's natural you'll want to spend time with your children, set aside time to be with them. Tell your older children when you'll be available to run errands, make meals, or entertain them.

PETS AND THE HOME OFFICE

If you work at home, a pet is a great companion. A dog or cat makes working at home less lonely. But as someone who's had a dog in my own home office for years, there are some important tips to making the most of a canine colleague.

- **Barking:** Just as you can't have a screaming child in the background, you can't have a barking dog — at least not too often. If your dog barks uncontrollably, put them in another room.

- **Walking:** Dog walking is an excellent way to meet new people, some of whom might be great networking contacts. I got my very first client walking my last dog, Teddy, in Golden Gate Park in San Francisco. Teddy, a grey terrier mix, intro-duced himself to a King Charles Spaniel, and his owner happened to need a business plan. Voila! My consulting service was launched.

- **Responsibilities**: If you work alone, give you dog a "position" in the company. I made Teddy my director of marketing. He took his job seriously, and over the years brought me many additional clients.

If you work too much, a dog is a great reason to take a break and go for a walk. Anyway, I love dogs. Even after I rented an office, I made sure the landlord would allow dogs. My dog, Cosmo, has his own bed right under my desk. And he's working his way up to a vice president's job.

Summary

Working at home can be a great advantage but it also presents some challenges, especially if you have children or spouses there, too. Planning your home office — its space, storage, and policies — helps you make the most of this arrangement. And don't forget your car! If you work from a vehicle, plan that "office," too.

MY WILD IDEAS FOR MY HOME OFFICE

e-business

This chapter is for those who actually conduct commerce on the Internet — selling products or services directly. Other issues of having a business presence on the Internet, such as using the Net for customer communication, intranets, etc., are covered in the Technology and Communication chapter.

Doing business on the Internet is still very much a pioneering enterprise — and will be for many years to come. The Internet world of e-commerce is constantly changing, with competitors coming and going, and technology continually evolving and improving.

In developing an Internet business, you will have to deal with "front-end issues" — what does the site itself look like, what's the nature of the user experience, what features do you offer — and "back-end issues" — how does everything all work, and what technology will you use for order fulfillment, inventory control, and other functions

Internet doesn't change business fundamentals. Customers still need a compelling reason to come to you, and once there, they need a compelling reason to buy and to return.

In fact, doing business on the Internet offers some greater challenges than doing business in the "real" world. With over 100 million websites, yours may be hard to find. On the Internet you have even more potential competitors than opening a store in a mall. Since customers never see you face-to-face, it's harder to establish trust and develop a loyal client base. And then there are all the issues of technology!

If you expect your website to be a success, you're going to have to put time, money, and most especially planning into making it work

Use the worksheet on page 197 to identify factors that contribute to making an Internet business a success and list some steps you'll take to achieve those goals.

HOW IS E-BUSINESS DIFFERENT?

I'm a big believer in the Internet. The Internet offers many opportunities and makes it possible for even small companies to do business worldwide. But the

GETTING AND KEEPING CUSTOMERS

Running a business on the Internet presents a unique challenge: how do you create a bond with your customers when they do not interact with you

RED TAPE ALERT!

When you run an offline company, you can control the key to your front door. In an online company, a lot of other people have the "keys" too. Make certain you always have the ultimate control over access to your data; know the passwords to all your databases at all times, and make certain that in your contract with providers or employees, passwords can not be changed without your authorization. List yourself as the administrative/final contact on your domain name registration, so that no one else can hold it hostage. If another company hosts your site, have a current backup of everything on your own computers, so if they suddenly go out of business, you don't also.

in any physical way? How do you create a welcoming environment for your customers when there is no environment? Moreover, in a situation where relatively little can be discerned about you by the customer — they can't see your offices, your store, your employees — building a relationship of trust is even more important than in the 'real' world.

Some of the factors that enhance the quality of the user's experience and increase their trust in you (and therefore, their willingness to do business with you) include:

- **Brand name/strategic partners.** Customers still seek name brands. If your company already has a brand name "offline," leverage that name to your Internet presence. If you don't have a brand name, find ways to offer name-brand products or have strategic partnerships with brand name companies

- **Quality of the site.** Just as a customer judges a retail store by the location, décor, furnishings, etc., a visitor to an Internet site determines how they feel about you by the quality of their experience. Are the graphics pleasing, the site well-designed and easy-to-use? Does the technology work?

- **Quality of order fulfillment and customer service.** To a customer, perhaps the most important factor of all is whether they get what they ordered on time. Since receiving an order may be the customer's only physical contact with the company, one bad experience can end a relationship with a customer forever.

- **Ability for customers to reach someone.** When all else fails, people want to talk to people.

Providing a way for customers to reach a real human being, whether to solve any problems, ask questions, or make a complaint, is extremely reassuring.

- **Being "certified."** Some organizations and businesses now provide screening procedures by which they will "certify" your site based on their criteria. Such criteria may relate to the physical existence of your company, your legal and financial status, or your privacy policies. Two such certification programs are run by the Better Business Bureau — the BBBOnline Privacy program and the BBBOnline Reliability program. You can find more about them at www.bbbonline.com.

Driving Traffic

You can't make sales if you don't get customers. Putting up a website doesn't mean users will necessarily find you. You have to market your Internet business just as you would your own real world business.

But how?

Some means are the same as those you would use in the offline world — taking out ads describing your site and products, putting your name and Internet address (url) on packages and products that you sell offline, getting publicity. All of these are effective and can be used to get people to know about your site.

But some means are unique to the Internet. While search engines will automatically list sites by topic, your site may not come up on a user's search, or may be so far down the list that no user will find it.

WHAT IS E-BUSINESS SUCCESS?

Success in e-business is not much different than success in any offline business — repeat customers, contented employees, and profits. However, e-businesses follow some different steps to achieve this success. Use this worksheet to consider how you will attract, motivate, and retain customers.

✔	Success Factor	Steps To Achieve This
	Attract the users you want.	
	Motivate users to take desired action.	
	Design a site that is easy to navigate.	
	Assure transactions can be completed satisfactorily.	
	Ship users' goods/services on time.	
	Motivate users to return, and to trust doing business with you.	
	Retain the customer and communicate with them again.	
	Other:	

Instead, you have to use various methods to improve the likelihood your site will be listed when a user puts a certain word or phrase in a search engine. If you're running an Internet company, you'll want to become familiar with some of these methods. Each search engine has its own criteria and methods for locating sites.

You can also increase the chance of being found through the use of "metatags" or keywords inserted in the code of your site. This helps search engines know which terms to use in relation to your site.

Online you can also advertise on other sites, develop strategic relationships so that other sites link to you without charge, or develop a partnership where your business is located on — or serves — a more highly visited site.

Use the worksheet on page 199 to list ways you can increase traffic to your site.

MAKING SALES

Once you've attracted users to your site, you want to turn those people who are merely looking into customers who actually buy. To do so, you need to design your site so that users can easily find the products or services they're looking for, understand the benefits and features, know the price, and place orders.

- **Site design and usability.** Websites are non-linear — customers don't go through a site step by step, but rather jump from place to place. It's easy for customers to get lost. Design your site — its overall architecture, 'look and feel,' and features — so users easily find what they need. And then make the process of buying clear and simple. Lay out your site to minimize the number of clicks it takes for a user to get what they want. Test your user interface to make certain potential customers understand how to use it, and add features — such as "shopping carts" — to make it easier for customers to buy.

- **Merchandising.** Just as in the offline world, customers to your online store need to have a good shopping experience. Design your site and navigation so users feel they've found a reputable dealer, enjoy being there, and feel motivated to purchase. Think about which products or services you want to feature on the home page, and how you will "rotate" merchandise so that frequent visitors find new things to buy.

- **Offline availability.** The most successful Internet e-commerce companies enable customers to reach a live human being via phone easily. Many shoppers use the Internet for research, but make their actual purchases offline. Integrate telephone support into your e-business, or at least list a phone number customers can use to reach a real person to take an order or answer questions.

- **"Stickiness."** The longer someone stays on your site, the more likely they are to buy and to want to return. Look for positive ways to encourage customers to spend more time with you — provide additional information, photos, customer reviews, or interactivity.

- **Add-on sales.** Customers may come to your site knowing exactly what they want to buy, but you can prompt them to buy more. Programming your software to suggest related products or services when a customer selects a product can increase your sales. Consider "bundling" to offer more products or services together for one set price.

Use the worksheet "Front-End Issues" on pages 202–203 to list ways you might be able to increase your actual sales.

Order Fulfillment and Customer Service

Everything in your company depends on your customer having a positive experience when they buy from you. Choose your software and hardware based on what you need to fulfill orders accurately and on time, and to be responsive to your customers. Customer service, inventory management, and order fulfillment are interrelated. Ideally, your database is designed so that customers know whether a product is in stock before they order, each customer order is

MY PLAN FOR DRIVING TRAFFIC

List steps you can take in each area to increase traffic to your site

✔	Strategy	Specifics
	Put your site name on offline products	
	Advertise offline	
	List on search engines	
	Secure Links/relationships with other sites	
	Increase public relations/publicity	
	Use "metatags"	
	Advertise Online	
	Other:	
	Other:	

then reflected in inventory, and the fulfillment process begins immediately.

If you are dealing with a tangible product, your order fulfillment process will involve third parties. You'll work with delivery services, such as FedEx, or suppliers and warehousers of finished goods, fulfillment houses (companies that warehouse and ship orders for you). Part of your planning process for an e-commerce business entails identifying the necessary third parties and negotiating arrangements with them.

In addition, consider the following issues in how your e-business interacts with customers, orders, and customer data:

- **Customer contact/e-mail.** An important part of your business development is staying in touch with customers. This may only be a matter of letting them know when an order is placed or shipped, or if there's a problem. But you may also want to design ways to communicate with customers on an ongoing basis to encourage them to return to your site. Mass e-mailings to update customers are a good way to stay in touch, as is sending personal e-mails to individual customers to let them know when you have new products or services of interest to them.

- **Security.** When you use the Internet, you want the information you provide to others to be kept private and secure. When you run your own site, you'll want to make the same assurances to your users. To do that, work with your website hosting company or internal technology staff to build in security procedures so that customer data is rea-

sonably secure from hackers. One type of security you'll want to provide is a secure connection between your user and your site when they provide personal or financial information (such as credit card numbers). You'll also want to make certain that only a limited number of highly trustworthy employees have access to customers' data.

- **Privacy.** How will you treat and respect the information your customers give you? Some companies share their data with others or even sell their data. Most users prefer to have their data kept entirely private — so they can control information about them. Whatever you choose, make certain your privacy policies are clearly stated in a visible place on your site before users give you such data. You may want to turn to the Better Business Bureau Online (www.bbbonline.com) to follow their privacy guidelines and qualify for their privacy seal.

- **Reliability.** If your site is not technically reliable — or features of your site are unreliable — you're going to lose customers. If your customers come to your site but key features, such as the ability to actually make purchases, don't work, they will probably never return. Worse yet, if your business is critical to a customer (you store their data, provide e-mail or Internet access, or are a vital supplier), and your site goes down, you're going to make some people very angry.

There's another type of reliability — being a reputable company yourself. Customers want to know that they're dealing with a company that will send their orders, follow privacy guarantees, and resolve

WHAT WOULD RHONDA DO . . . TO RUN AN E-BUSINESS

First, I'd do my homework. I'd learn as much as I could about how e-commerce works: what succeeds, what doesn't. I'd research other websites selling similar products or services — and buy from them to see how well they perform. I'd learn the fundamentals of the technology I'm going to rely on for my business. Then I'd get the best tech help I could afford — a consultant, advisor, or employee, and I'd really listen to them. I wouldn't allow myself to think I know everything, and I wouldn't allow myself to be in a position where I know nothing. I'd use off-the-shelf solutions whenever possible: I might not get all the bells-and-whistles, but it wouldn't cost as much money, and I could get it up and running faster. I'd make my business goals realistic, and I'd try to keep things as simple as possible.

disputes or complaints. Make certain that customers have an off line way to reach you, and once again, you may want to qualify for the Better Business Bureau's "Reliability" seal to reassure customers.

Working Globally

You may be physically located on Main Street, USA, but when you do business on the Internet, you can potentially have customers around the world. But just because you're on the Internet doesn't mean that the real-world differences and challenges of doing business internationally have disappeared.

The biggest challenges come if you're sending a physical product. You'll need to deal with customs, collections, and returns. If you intend to do a great deal of international sales, you need to fully address these issues. If you only occasionally make an international sale, think about a few issues before you send your product, including:

- How do you receive payment? In what currency?
- Who pays shipping and custom charges?
- How do you guarantee timely delivery?
- How will you handle returns? Who pays?
- How do you resolve complaints?

Even if you don't ship a physical product, but instead offer a service or downloadable software, you'll face a few issues when dealing with customers from other countries. The biggest may relate to language. You may need to translate all or a portion of your site into other languages and/or provide international phone numbers.

THE BACK-END TECHNICAL STUFF

To run an e-business, you don't necessarily need to know how to write software programs or fix a computer, but you have to know enough to hire the right people or consulting firms to do those things, and to participate in discussions and make critical business decisions affecting the future of your company. If you're not already comfortable discussing technology, you'll have to familiarize yourself with key issues and terms.

Since every e-business has different technical issues, and technology solutions continually change, only a few key technical concerns are discussed here. For issues specific to your site and business, you may

QUESTIONS TO ASK . . . A SITE HOSTING PROVIDER

- What kinds of sites do they serve most? Are they primarily dedicated to companies like yours or other types of sites (such as personal sites or sites for big businesses)?
- How long have they been in business? How are they funded?
- What guarantees of technical support do you have? Do you have telephone access as well as online support? What hours? Days?
- What platform/server do they offer?
- What services are included in the basic cost? What additional services are offered?
- How do they protect the privacy and security of data?
- What kind of reports can they generate?
- What kind of backup do they provide?
- What kind of Internet connection do they provide? Do they have redundant connections?
- What is their "uptime" guarantee?
- Do they monitor their servers 24/7? What level of performance do they promise to provide (how many sites on a server, speed, etc.)?

FRONT-END ISSUES

Describe the key features that will distinguish your e-business' front-end.

Quality of User Experience	Design Specifics
Site design pleasing and appropriate to my target market.	
Site map/navigation aids	
Number of user clicks to make a purchase	
"Stickiness" — features that keep customers at the site and encourage them to return	
Prompts encouraging customers to buy	
Prompts encouraging additional purchases	
Internet connection speed of your target market vs. speed for optimum enjoyment of your site	
Consistency of site design with different browsers and at different connection speeds	
How have users reacted when you tested the design and functions with them?	

FRONT-END ISSUES (CONTINUED)

Indicate the specifics of each site feature and mark whether it is: A – Absolutely Necessary, D – Desirable, or N – Not Necessary

Feature	Specifics	How Necessary?
Ability to reach live service rep		
Advanced search capabilities		
Personalization		
Registration		
Shopping cart		
Security		
Storing customer preferences		
Storing customer payment info		
Real-time inventory information		
Prompts of related items		
Customer reviews and product ratings		
Other:		
Other:		
Other:		

QUESTIONS TO ASK . . . A TECHNICAL CONSULTANT

- Have you worked for similar businesses before?
- Have you worked for an e-commerce company before? What did you do for them?
- Have you ever designed and built an e-commerce website? What aspects of a website were you responsible for?
- What software do you have experience with?
- What platforms do you work with: Unix, Linux, Microsoft, other?
- What database programs do you work with?
- What kinds of certification do you have?
- What programming experience do you have?
- Have you designed and administered a database? What did it do?
- Have you set up a network?
- Have you ever set up and administered a web server?
- Have you set up a back-end system combining online activities with back end financial records, credit card processing, inventory management, or customer relationship management?
- What experience do you have with online marketing, such as increasing visibility on search engines, doing mass e-mails, etc.?

want to turn to technical consultants or the support staff of your site hosting company. Use the "Questions to Ask . . ." guides on pages 201 and 204 when you begin interviewing or hiring this outside technical help.

Back-end issues you'll face in setting up and developing your website are:

- **Platform.** Choosing a platform is perhaps the most critical technology question because it is the basic operating system you'll use to run your company. And once you've chosen a platform, it's difficult and expensive to change. Some platforms, such as Unix, provide greater growth potential and can handle larger volumes of traffic, but they're more complicated and/or expensive to run (hardware, software, and consultants) than others, while other platforms, such as Microsoft may be easier and cost less. Carefully weigh the pros and cons of each platform and how it fits with your company's current capabilities and future needs.

- **In-house versus "off-the-shelf."** One of the questions you'll face repeatedly is whether to buy "off-the-shelf" software programs, to customize such software, or to build software from scratch. The advantage of having customized or in-house developed software is that it can be designed specifically for your needs and may provide you a competitive advantage against the competition. The disadvantage is that it's far more costly, more time-consuming, less compatible with other programs, and more specialized in the technical staff needed to maintain it in the future.

- **Hosting.** Will you host your site yourself or use an outside hosting service? Key considerations here are what kind of Internet connections you have and the level of technical resources you possess. There are many advantages to using outside services, including faster, multiple connections to the Internet, ensuring that if one connection goes down, your site can still operate. Outside services are more likely to provide 'round-the-clock server maintenance and technical support. Choose a host carefully, and check a number of options. Don't just look at their website, but call and talk to an actual person and find out about how dedicated they are to businesses like yours. Get the telephone number of the tech support help line and call at different times to see how long you have to wait or if someone answers.

Use the worksheet "Back-End Issues" on pages 206–207 to outline the issues your e-business faces, and work with your technical support staff, whether in-house or outsourced, to develop solutions that work for your business.

Summary

The Internet has opened up amazing opportunities, and you may want to take advantage of these by selling your products or services online. You may be able to vastly increase your customer base, finding customers across the globe.

But the Internet does not change business fundamentals. You still have to have a compelling business proposition — products or services customers need or want to buy at a price they can afford. And you must be able to deliver what you promise and keep the customers you attract. You also have to understand the technology that your company depends upon; if you are running the company, you must make yourself familiar with key technology issues and terms.

Remember, an Internet business is still a "business." You have to make money the old-fashioned way: earning it!

BACK-END ISSUES

Hardware

What platform will you use?

What database will you use?

Where will your technology staff come from: in-house or outsource? Specify:

Software

Will you develop software in-house, buy off-the-shelf, or customize off-the-shelf products? Specify:

How will Internet purchases/activities integrate with your current database/inventory systems/software?

Below, list your key software programs, and determine its functionality, from compatibility to overall reliability:

Name of Key Software:			
Functionality			
Compatibility			
Expandability/Scaleability			
Cost			
Hardware Cost			
Installation Time			
Support Staff Required			
Maintenance			
Ability to Handle Traffic Surges			
Overall Reliability			

BACK-END ISSUES

Inventory
Where will your inventory come from?
Where will your inventory be warehoused?
Who will do order fulfillment: packing, shipping, etc?
Will you provide real time inventory information? ☐ Yes ☐ No If so, how will the customer know at time of purchase if product is available and how will you manage that service?

Indicate third party arrangements you'll need or have lined up, and specifics:

Suppliers:	
Warehouse:	
Order fulfillment	
Delivery services:	
Customer service/ Tech support:	
Other:	
Other:	

MY WILD IDEAS FOR MY E-BUSINESS

crisis center

Here is one thing I can absolutely promise you: things will go wrong. At some point, something unexpected will affect your business — there will be a natural disaster, your computer will crash, your main supplier will suddenly go out of business. Even more likely, your printer will run out of ink when you're on deadline, a key employee will be sick when you're in the midst of a big project, or the projector won't work when you've got a presentation to a major client. Bad things do happen to good companies.

CONTINGENCY PLANNING

To help prepare for an emergency or crisis, first figure out what kind of crisis your business is likely to face and what would be critical if that occurred. Begin by listing the types of emergencies that could reasonably affect you, and the potential effects of that emergency. Use the worksheet on page 210.

Next, for a two week period, keep notes on how you conduct your business on a day-to-day basis to better understand what you absolutely depend on to stay in business. Keep track of the equipment you depend on, the computer files you absolutely must have, and what would happen if you didn't have access to your equipment, certain employees, or your

building. If your business is telephone dependent, how would you get your messages or respond? What about online access? Do you know how to reroute or pick up your e-mail if an emergency knocked out your computers?

Remember, a disaster elsewhere may also be a disaster for you, especially if your business depends on distant key suppliers. Develop a list of alternatives in case your regular supplier becomes unavailable.

After you've considered the vital systems, people, and access you need during that two-week period, use the "Contingency Plan" worksheet on page 212 to determine how to meet your critical business needs.

NATURAL DISASTERS

Hurricanes, fire, storms. It's always something! I've had my business interrupted by two natural disasters — an earthquake and a flood. But I've been lucky; all I've ever lost was power and a few days work. Others will not be so fortunate: they'll lose inventory, customer records, equipment.

When disaster strikes your business, you'll be glad you developed an emergency preparedness plan.

WHAT TYPE OF EMERGENCIES MIGHT I FACE?

Emergency Type	Likelihood	Effects	Steps to Mitigate
Fire			
Flood/storm			
Earthquake/hurricane			
Theft/embezzlement			
Absence of key employee			
Loss of electricity			
Computer failure			
Other equipment failure			
Sudden loss of major supplier			
Sudden loss of major customer			
Other			

Taking a few simple steps can save you a lot of money and heartache.

The kinds of preparations you make depend on the dangers your location is likely to face. Bolting down bookshelves (to protect against earthquake) may be more important in San Francisco than Chicago, while a Chicago area business might do well to consider steps to mitigate the effects of a major snowstorm — not a concern in San Francisco at all. Take steps to mitigate the effects of natural occurrences that might affect your business.

Any business could be affected by fire, and all companies should try to reduce that likelihood. Of course, if your company is particularly exposed to fire — you deal with hazardous or highly flammable materials, work in an old building, or are located in a high fire-danger area — work with the fire department or fire prevention experts to help develop fire prevention and emergency plans.

In a serious disaster, the most important thing is safety: for yourself, employees, and customers. Develop evacuation plans, make certain employees know what to do in emergencies, and conduct safety and fire drills. Know how to get out of your building and where to go.

After a natural disaster strikes, it may be difficult to reach employees since phone lines often go down. Develop an emergency contact plan, list alternative contact phone numbers, and decide how employees will be notified of developments. Use the worksheet on page 218–219 to list alternate phone numbers for employees in case of emergency. In addition, the worksheet on page 210 provides space to list the kinds of natural disasters that might affect your company and the steps you can take to mitigate consequences.

WILL INSURANCE PROTECT ME?

The place to start when planning to mitigate the effects of catastrophe is insurance. As awful as a disaster can be, it can be less devastating if insurance covers the financial losses and helps you get going again.

Of course, you must begin with the basics: fire, theft, liability. If your business is likely to be affected by a natural disaster, consider disaster insurance as well. While it can be very expensive, it should be evaluated just as any other business expense.

Also consider "business interruption insurance." This covers you even if your business doesn't suffer physical damage but does lose income due to the effects of a disaster, such as closed roads, making it impossible for customers to reach you.

If you run a home-based business, look at your policies closely and talk to your insurance broker. Most homeowner policies (for fire and theft) don't cover things such as computers, tools, samples, and you'll want to add additional coverage to protect you against those losses.

Use the worksheet on page 137 of the Operations chapter to list the kinds of insurance your company needs.

COMPUTERS, EQUIPMENT, AND DATA

Even more likely than a natural disaster striking your company is the possibility of a computer disaster hitting. I've had two hard drives crash. Believe me, it's not something you want to experience — and it's a lot less damaging if you have a full backup of data.

Make Backups!

Backing up your computer records and database is vital, but it's also important to store a copy off-site. Small companies can have the boss or a key employee take a copy home once a week; that way, at any given time, a set of records is safe at another location and no more than one week's worth of work can be lost. When I wrote my first book, once a week I took a backup copy of my disk to a neighbor's. Wrong! Store backups at least a mile away; in a fire, a neighbor may also be in trouble.

CONTINGENCY PLAN

Use this worksheet to keep track of those things you depend on for a two week period.

What	How/Who You Depend On	Backup Alternatives?
Access to offices/building		
Access to customer/ financial accounts		
Access to other information		
Processing orders		
Handling phone calls		
Producing product/service		
Shipping/receiving		
Access to Electricity		
Access to Phones		
Access to Internet		
Other		
Other		

Another alternative for off-site storage is to use an online backup company where your data is sent every evening (or more often) over the Internet for storage. Bigger companies may want to build redundant computer systems to keep records at distant locations.

An easy and quick prevention is to get a fireproof safe for vital documents and purchase a backup power supply. Both safes and inexpensive power backup generators are available at office supply stores. You'll get about a half hour's power in case of power loss, giving you time to back up records.

If you run an Internet company, make certain your website hosting company has backup access to the Internet and redundant equipment. You don't want your company to be shut down for days because your ISP has been struck with a snowstorm. You also don't want to be left high and dry if they suddenly go out of business or your tech consultant moves. The key is always to have backups and alternatives.

Use the worksheet below to develop backup procedures for your data and equipment and to identify backup alternatives for lack of access to communication or people.

Technical Support

Trust me, sooner or later you're going to need help figuring out how to make something work. You're going to ask a fellow employee, call your brother-in-law or contact a technical support hotline.

Prepare for these conversations by developing your own technical support procedures. Start with the worksheet "My Own FAQ's" on page 215 to list answers to the questions you ask repeatedly — how to reset your computer, your settings for your Internet provider, steps to take when backing up, etc. You'll know what these questions are — the second or third time you've asked them. Write down the answers here!

Next, keep a list of technical support contact numbers and e-mail handy. Use the tech support contact worksheet on page 216 to keep the data you need available when you have to make that phone call.

Finally, once you've reached technical support, keep track of who you've talked to and what they've advised. Unfortunately, the first call may not always solve the problem, and you'll want to be able to call the same person back or verify the information you

BACKUP PLAN

Use this worksheet to plan how often you'll make backups, where you'll store them, and who will be responsible.

What	Backup Alternatives or Schedule
Financial Data	
Customer Records	
Administrative Records	
Other Data:	
Other Data:	

received the first time. The "Tech Support History" worksheet on page 217 helps you record these conversations.

ABSENCE OF KEY EMPLOYEES

Emergencies also come in the form of personal disasters, such as illnesses and accidents, so develop back-up procedures in case you or key employees become unavailable. Make certain someone knows where your records are and has the power to deposit checks, pay pressing bills, and contact customers. This could be a key employee, an attorney, even a family member. Just make sure you trust them!

Also make certain other people have physical access to your offices and data. If you're the only person with keys to your building or knowledge of your passwords, what will happen if you're unavailable?

On the other hand, if other employees have access to passwords to your database, records or other critical data, make sure that you also have those passwords and give approval and get notice whenever passwords are changed. You don't want your data to be captive of other employees.

Summary

You can't entirely prevent a crisis from hitting you and your company, but by taking a few precautions you can mitigate some of the worst effects. The key is usually backup — systems, access, data, support, employees.

Finally, keep in mind that disasters have psychological as well as physical and financial effects. You and your employees will need time to readjust, so expect some distractions and extra time spent around the water cooler recounting just where they were when the dam broke, the tornado struck, or the earth shook. Stay safe!

MY OWN FAQ'S

Use this sheet to list the answers to technical questions you ask frequently.

Problems/Questions	Answer

TECH SUPPORT CONTACTS

Keep this list handy. Make copies for all potentially affected employees.

Product	Registration #
Date product purchased	Additional tech support purchased?
Tech Support Phone #	Fax#
Website	E-mail
Address	Name

Product	Registration #
Date product purchased	Additional tech support purchased?
Tech Support Phone #	Fax#
Website	E-mail
Address	Name

Product	Registration #
Date product purchased	Additional tech support purchased?
Tech Support Phone #	Fax#
Website	E-mail
Address	Name

Product	Registration #
Date product purchased	Additional tech support purchased?
Tech Support Phone #	Fax#
Website	E-mail
Address	Name

Product	Registration #
Date product purchased	Additional tech support purchased?
Tech Support Phone #	Fax#
Website	E-mail
Address	Name

Product	Registration #
Date product purchased	Additional tech support purchased?
Tech Support Phone #	Fax#
Website	E-mail
Address	Name

TECH SUPPORT HISTORY

Keep track of your contacts to technical support, so you can refer back on future calls.

Tech Support Call:	Date called:
Person talked to:	Their direct contact info:
Phone/E-mail:	Issue/Concern:
Their response/direction:	
Other suggestions:	
Outcome:	

Tech Support Call:	Date called:
Person talked to:	Their direct contact info:
Phone/E-mail:	Issue/Concern:
Their response/direction:	
Other suggestions:	
Outcome:	

Tech Support Call:	Date called:
Person talked to:	Their direct contact info:
Phone/E-mail:	Issue/Concern:
Their response/direction:	
Other suggestions:	
Outcome:	

Tech Support Call:	Date called:
Person talked to:	Their direct contact info:
Phone/E-mail:	Issue/Concern:
Their response/direction:	
Other suggestions:	
Outcome:	

Tech Support Call:	Date called:
Person talked to:	Their direct contact info:
Phone/E-mail:	Issue/Concern:
Their response/direction:	
Other suggestions:	
Outcome:	

CONTACT SHEET: EMERGENCY PHONE NUMBERS

In case of emergency, list additional phone numbers for employees – or key customers or suppliers.

Name	Home Number	Cell Phone Number	First Alternate Number/Contact	Second Alternate Number/Contact

EMERGENCY CONTACTS (CONTINUED)

Name	Home Number	Cell Phone Number	First Alternate Number/Contact	Second Alternate Number/Contact

MY WILD IDEAS FOR CRISIS MANAGEMENT

resources

Use the following pages to help plan your additional, specific needs. Keep track of your contacts on the contact list provided and use the Comparison Charts and Shopping Lists for further shopping or researching of products or services. The file folder labels will help you set up a system for keeping your data organized.

The Outline of a Business Plan and Glossary are additional tools for you as your business grows.

COMPARISON CHART		
QUESTIONS	OPTION 1	OPTION 2

COMPARISON CHART

OPTION 3	OPTION 4	OPTION 5

MY SHOPPING LIST

MY SHOPPING LIST

CONTACTS

Name:

Company:

Address:

Phone:

Fax:

E-mail:

Web Address:

Notes:

Name:

Company:

Address:

Phone:

Fax:

E-mail:

Web Address:

Notes:

Name:

Company:

Address:

Phone:

Fax:

E-mail:

Web Address:

Notes:

Name:

Company:

Address:

Phone:

Fax:

E-mail:

Web Address:

Notes:

Name:

Company:

Address:

Phone:

Fax:

E-mail:

Web Address:

Notes:

Name:

Company:

Address:

Phone:

Fax:

E-mail:

Web Address:

Notes:

CONTACTS

Name:

Company:

Address:

Phone:

Fax:

E-mail:

Web Address:

Notes:

Name:

Company:

Address:

Phone:

Fax:

E-mail:

Web Address:

Notes:

Name:

Company:

Address:

Phone:

Fax:

E-mail:

Web Address:

Notes:

Name:

Company:

Address:

Phone:

Fax:

E-mail:

Web Address:

Notes:

Name:

Company:

Address:

Phone:

Fax:

E-mail:

Web Address:

Notes:

Name:

Company:

Address:

Phone:

Fax:

E-mail:

Web Address:

Notes:

CONTACTS

Name:

Company:

Address:

Phone:

Fax:

E-mail:

Web Address:

Notes:

Name:

Company:

Address:

Phone:

Fax:

E-mail:

Web Address:

Notes:

Name:

Company:

Address:

Phone:

Fax:

E-mail:

Web Address:

Notes:

Name:

Company:

Address:

Phone:

Fax:

E-mail:

Web Address:

Notes:

Name:

Company:

Address:

Phone:

Fax:

E-mail:

Web Address:

Notes:

Name:

Company:

Address:

Phone:

Fax:

E-mail:

Web Address:

Notes:

CONTACTS

Name:

Company:

Address:

Phone:

Fax:

E-mail:

Web Address:

Notes:

Name:

Company:

Address:

Phone:

Fax:

E-mail:

Web Address:

Notes:

Name:

Company:

Address:

Phone:

Fax:

E-mail:

Web Address:

Notes:

Name:

Company:

Address:

Phone:

Fax:

E-mail:

Web Address:

Notes:

Name:

Company:

Address:

Phone:

Fax:

E-mail:

Web Address:

Notes:

Name:

Company:

Address:

Phone:

Fax:

E-mail:

Web Address:

Notes:

QUESTIONS TO ASK...

As you start and grow your business, you'll rely on the help of others. Never be afraid to ask them the questions that are on your mind. I've provided some guidelines throughout the book of questions to ask the people you'll be working with. Use this space to make notes of other questions you've formulated on your own. The old saying still holds true: the only stupid question is the one that's never asked.

Questions to Ask . . .

FILE FOLDER LABELS

Cut out these labels and fold them in half. Then, insert them into plastic tabs for hanging file folders.

Accountant	Distributors	Loans
Accounts Payable (Bills)	Entertainment / Meals	Market Research
Accounts Receivable (Invoices)	Equipment/ Technology	Mileage / Parking
Advertising	Insurance	Names/ Trademarks
Bank Accounts	Investors	Payroll
Contracts — Customers	Lawyer	Suppliers
Contracts — Employees	Lease	Tax Matters
Customers: Potential	Licenses	Travel

outline of a business plan

This is taken from The Successful Business Plan: Secrets and Strategies, *also by Rhonda Abrams, which is a step-by-step guide to developing your business plan.*

I. **Executive Summary**

II. **Company Description**
  A. Legal Name and Form of Business
  B. Mission Statement/Objectives
  C. Names of Top Management
  D. Location and Geographical Information
  E. Company's Development Stage
  F. Trademarks, Copyrights & Other Legal
  G. Company Products or Services
  H. Specialty Business Information
  I. Financial Status
  J. Milestones Achieved to Date

III. **Industry Analysis and Trends**
  A. Size and Growth
  B. Maturity of Industry
  C. Vulnerability to Economic Factors
  D. Seasonal Factors
  E. Technological Factors
  F. Regulatory Issues
  G. Supply and Distribution
  H. Financial Considerations
  I. Anticipated Changes & Trends in Industry

IV. **The Target Market**

A. Demographics/Geographics
B. Lifestyle and Psychographics
C. Purchasing Patterns
D. Buying Sensitivities
E. Size and Trends of Market

V. The Competition
A. Competitive Position
B. Market Share Distribution
C. Barriers to Entry
D. Future Competition

VI. Strategic Position & Risk Assessment
A. Company Strengths
B. Market/Industry Opportunities
C. Risks Assessment
D. Definition of Strategic Position

VII. Marketing Plan and Sales Strategy
A. Company's Message
B. Marketing Vehicles
C. Strategic Partnerships
D. Other Marketing Tactics
E. Sales Force and Structure
F. Sales Assumptions

VIII. Operations
A. Plant and Facilities
B. Manufacturing/Production Plan
C. Equipment and Technology
D. Variable Labor Requirements
E. Inventory Management
F. Supply and Distribution
G. Order Fulfillment and Customer Service
H. Research and Development
I. Capacity Utilization
J. Quality Control
K. Safety, Health, and Environmental Concerns
L. Shrinkage
M. Management Information Systems
N. Other Operational Concerns

IX. Technology Plan
A. Technology Goals and Position
B. Internet Goals and Plan
C. Hardware Needs
D. Software Needs

    E. Telecommunications Needs

    F. Personnel Needs

X. Management and Organization

    A. Principals/Key Employees

    B. Board of Directors

    C. Consultants/Specialists

    D. Management to Be Added

    E. Organizational Chart

    F. Management Style/Corporate Culture

XI. Community Involvement & Social Responsibility

    A. Social Responsibility Goals

    B. Company Policies

    C. Community Activities

XII. Development, Milestones & Exit Plan

    A. Long-Term Company Goals

    B. Growth Strategy

    C. Milestones

    D. Risk Evaluation

    E. Exit Plan

XIII. The Financials

    A. Income Statement

    B. Cash Flow

    C. Balance Sheet

    D. Break-Even Analysis (if desired)

    E. Plan Assumptions

    F. Uses of Funds

XIV. Appendix

glossary

24/7. Twenty-four hours a day, seven days a week. A term used to describe a service, Internet site, or other activity that is continually available.

Accrual Based Accounting. An accounting method whereby income and expenses are entered on the books at the time of contract or agreement rather than at the time of payment or receipt of funds.

Advisory Board. A non-official group of advisors; has no legal authority or obligation.

Angel. A private individual who invests their own money in new enterprises.

Barriers to Entry. Those conditions that make it difficult or impossible for new competitors to enter the market: two barriers to entry are patents and high start-up costs.

Board of Directors. The members of the governing body of an incorporated company. They have legal responsibility for the company.

Capacity. The amount of goods or work that can be produced by a company given its level of equipment, labor, and facilities.

Capital. The funds necessary to establish or operate a business.

Cash Based Accounting. An accounting method whereby income and expenses are entered on the books at the time of actual payment or receipt of funds.

Cash Flow. The movement of money into and out of a company; actual income received and actual payments made out.

Collateral. Assets pledged in return for loans.

Conventional Financing. Financing from established lenders, such as banks, rather than from investors; debt financing.

Convertible Debt. Loans made to a company that can be repaid with stock ownership (or a combination of stock and cash), usually at the lender's option.

dba. "Doing business as..." a company's trade name rather than the name by which it is legally incorporated; a company may be incorporated under the name XYZ Corporation but do business as "The Dew Drop Inn."

Debt Financing. Raising funds for a business by borrowing, often in the form of bank loans.

Debt Service. Money being paid on a loan; the amount necessary to keep a loan from going into default.

Deferred Compensation. Salary delayed until a future date; often taken by principal employees as a method of reducing expenditures in early years of operation.

Disbursements. Money paid out.

Distributor. Company or individual that arranges for the sale of products from manufacturer to retail outlets; the proverbial "middle man."

Downside Risk. The maximum amount that can be lost in an investment.

Due Diligence. The process undertaken by venture capitalists, investment bankers or others to thoroughly investigate a company before financing; required by law before offering securities for sale.

e-Business. A company that operates and exists primarily on the Internet.

e-Commerce. Conducting sales and transactions on the Internet.

Equity. Shares of stock in company; ownership interest in a company.

Event. Investors or others may speak of an "event" taking place, usually a time at which value can be liquidated from the company. Commonly a funding round, acquisition, or an IPO.

Exit Plan. The strategy for leaving an investment and realizing the profits of such investment.

Funding Rounds. The number of times a company goes to the investment community to seek financing; each funding round is used to reach new stages of company development.

"Going Public." To issue an IPO (see below).

Initial Public Offering (IPO). The first time the company's stock is sold to the general public (other than by a limited offering) through stock market or over-the-counter sales.

ISP: Internet Service Provider. A company that provides access to the Internet and/or hosts a company's Internet site.

Lead Investor. The individual or investment firm taking primary responsibility for the financing of a company; usually brings other investors or venture capital firms into the deal and monitors the investment for all.

Leasehold Improvements. The changes made to a rented store, office, or plant, to suit the tenant and make the location more appropriate for the conduct of the tenant's business.

Letter-of-Intent. A letter or other document by a customer indicating the customer's intention to buy from a company.

Licensing. The granting of permission by one company to another to use its products, trademark, or name in a limited, particular manner.

Limited Partnership. An investment method whereby investors have limited liability and exercise no control over a company or enterprise; the general partner(s) maintain control and liability.

Liquidity. The ability to turn assets into cash quickly and easily; widely-traded stocks are usually a liquid asset.

Manufacturing Companies. Businesses which make products from raw or unfinished materials generally to be sold to intermediaries (such as stores and dealers) rather than the end-user.

Market Share. The percentage of the total available customer base captured by a company.

Milestone. A particular business achievement by which a company can be judged.

Mind Share. A relative sense of the awareness level a company has achieved in its target market versus the recognition and awareness of its competition.

Net Worth. The total ownership interest in a company, represented by the excess of the total amount of assets minus the total amount of liabilities.

Options. The right to buy stock in a company at a later date, usually at a pre-set price; if the stock rises higher than the original price, an option holder is likely to exercise these options.

Outsource. To have certain tasks, jobs, manufacturing, etc. produced by another company on a contract basis rather than having the work done by one's own company "in-house."

Partnership. A legal relationship of two or more individuals to run a company.

Profit Margin. The amount of money earned after the cost of goods (gross profit margin) or all operating expenses (net profit margin) are deducted; usually expressed in percentage terms.

Proprietary Technology or Information. Technology or information belonging to a company; private information not to be disseminated to others.

Receipts. Funds coming in to the company; the actual money paid to the company for its products or services; not necessarily the same as a company's actual revenues.

Sole Proprietorship. Company owned and managed by one person.

Strategic Partnerships. An agreement with another company to undertake business endeavors together or on each other's behalf; can be for financing, sales, marketing, distribution, or other activities.

Term Sheet. A proposal by an investor of the terms on which they will make an investment in a company.

Traffic. When used for an Internet site, describes the amount of use, the number of visitors the site receives.

Venture Capitalist. Individual or firm who invests money in new enterprises; typically this is money invested in the venture capital firm by others, particularly institutional investors.

Working Capital. The cash available to the company for the on-going operations of the business.

index

Cut through the red tape jungle.

Sometimes running a business can seem overwhelming—all the complicated rules, regulations, and laws. Cut through the confusion with *Starting and Operating a Business in the U.S.* by Michael D. Jenkins.

State and federal laws, tax regulations, personnel management and responsibilities, accounting requirements, environmental laws, technology issues, and dozens of other important areas of business are all clearly outlined and explained in this best-selling companion guide to Rhonda Abrams' *The Successful Business Organizer* and *The Successful Business Plan*.

Jenkins packs the book with worksheets, checklists, forms, sources, and contact information to help you start and manage your growing business. A CD-ROM containing up-to-date state-specific business laws and information is also included.

"Anyone who is thinking of starting a business should read this book."
— Jack Farris, President,
  National Federation of
  Independent Business